IMPERIALISM AND ETHNIC
POLITICS IN NIGERIA

IMPERIALISM AND ETHNIC POLITICS IN NIGERIA,1960–96

PADE BADRU

Africa World Press, Inc.

P.O. Box 1892
Trenton, NJ 08607

P.O. Box 48
Asmara, ERITREA

Africa World Press, Inc.

P.O. Box 1892
Trenton, NJ 08607

P.O. Box 48
Asmara, ERITREA

Copyright © 1998 Pade Badru

First Printing 1998

Cover Design: Jonathan Gullery
Book Design: Wanjiku Ngugi

Library of Congress Cataloging-in-Publication Data

Badru, Pade.
    Imperialism and ethnic politics in Nigeria, 1960-1996 / Pade
Badru.
       p. cm.
    Includes bibliographical references (p.) and index.
    ISBN 0-86543-603-7 (cloth). -- ISBN 0-86543-604-5 (paper : alk.
paper)
    1. Nigeria-- Politics and government -- 1960- 2. Nigeria--Ethnic
relations--Political aspects--History--20th century. 3. Social
classes--Nigeria--History--20th century. 4. Military government-
-Nigeria--History--20th century. 5. Nigeria--Colonial influence-
-History--20th century. I. Title
DT515.8.B25 1997
966.905--dc21
                                  97-35162
                                       CIP

Contents

LIST OF TABLES

Acknowledgements

Without the unwavering support of several people in my life, this current work would not have been possible. First and foremost is my mother, Eniafolurunsho Efunwade-Oyediran, who passed away in September 4, 1996 shortly after the final data for this book were collected. It is my belief that her death was speeded up by the conditions created by the implementation of the IMF sponsored structural adjustment program in Nigeria, which made quality health provision inaccessible to the masses of Nigerian people. It is to her memory that this book is dedicated. I would also like to express my thanks to my colleagues at the University of Louisville for their support of my work, especially those in Pan African Studies. Finally, my thanks to Gary Hunter whose constant critiques and comments about Nigeria politics, during my year long visiting professorship at the Rowan University of New Jersey, made it possible for me to refine some of the ideas in this book.

Of course, I bear sole responsibility for the empirical and conceptual faults and errors.

Preface

The idea of this book was conceived in 1986 while I was teaching at the University of Port Harcourt in Nigeria. The time was particularly a difficult one given the ongoing national debate on the future of politics in Nigeria once the military junta relinquished political power. The debate was sarcastically disturbing because it was directly orchestrated and stage managed by the military government of General Ibrahim Babangida whose eight years in power was most devastating to the masses of Nigerians.

The lack of consistent opposition to the dictatorship itself revealed a national spirit that was buried under the rubrics of an understandable pessimism with regards to the survival of Nigeria as a united nation. The decision of the Academic Staff Union (ASU) and some radical intellectuals to participate in the debate was rather a puzzling one to some of us who thought that the idea of the debate should have been rejected. Instead of demanding the ouster of the military from power, especially after it had slaughtered innocent students who had objected to the debate and the government austerity measures, the leadership of ASU and the trade unions leadership, erroneously saw in the debate a signal on the part of the military junta to relinquish power.

More troubling too was the tone of the debate as many participants, nationally, conceded to the idea that Nigeria could not survive as a nation. These individuals cited ethnicity as a major impediment to Nigerian unity. Some of the proponents of this idea suggested a form of confederacy in which each ethnic group would exercise regional control over major political decisions that might affect its own interest. More absurd were the old politicians, especially the Yoruba elite, who went as far as to propose the breaking up of the country along ethnic lines, particularly along the north-south divide. The dominant analysis of the Nigerian crisis, by radical intellectuals and liberals alike, thus focused unduly on ethnicity as opposed to class.

But when one looks at the viciousness of the military regime of General Babangida and those of the regimes that preceded it, it is clear that ethnicity had very little to do with military rule, and that those that continued to play the ethnic card did so to achieve their own political agenda. Thus, the position of this writer is that the ruling elite, whether constituted in the military or civil society, consistently used ethnicity to secure its own class domination in the absence of a coherent class ideology.

The book contains nine chapters which all look at the interconnections of politics, economics, and ethnicity. The introductory chapter addresses the peculiar geography of Nigeria as a state and looks at the history of the Nigerian nationalist struggle as a precursor to decolonization. It then analyses the way ethnicity was used by the British imperial state, during the colonial and decolonization eras, to preempt attempts by the nationalist leaders at mobilizing the masses against colonial rule. In addition to this, the first chapter also examines the persistence of the dynamics of ethnicity in post-independence Nigeria, both in terms of its divisiveness in nation building, and in its primacy in terms of resource distribution and regional development.

In chapter two, several sociological and political science theories of the State are discussed in order to show how relevant or irrelevant those theories are to the Nigerian situation. The chapter examines, in particular, the whole question of the possibility of transforming the current neocolonial state into one that represents the economic and political aspirations of internal social classes as free people, as opposed to a state that continues to represent the interests of colonial exploiters. It focuses especially at the competition for the control of the state by the ethnically fragmented elites and the implication of this competition for nation building, ethnic identity, and continuing allegiance to primordial interests. In addition, the chapter goes on to examine how the fragmentation of the civilian elite allows for the persistence of military intervention culminating in the creation of a new class of military elite whose goal becomes increasingly the perpetuation of elite rule.

Chapter three examines the persisting economic crisis that makes the instability of the Nigerian state a necessary feature of underdevelopment. The chapter also examines the structure of the dependent economy and the rapid decline of the agricultural sector during the era of oil boom. It goes on to examine the problems faced by state bureaucrats in trying to pursue coherent development policies in the face of internal corruption and the monopolization of investible resources by multinational corporations. The final part of the chapter traces the origin of the Structural Adjustment Program (SAP) and its social and economic impact on the people.

In chapter four, the origins of military rule and the persistence of this particular form of class rule, are examined. The chapter argues that the inability of any stratum of the political class to exert its total control over the state allowed for the rise and persistence of military rule. This chapter further characterizes military rule as a unique political arrangement that is capable of generating the sort of social and political climate necessary for accumulation by international capital and its local representatives. The chapter takes the reader through the various military regimes since the first intervention in 1966.

Chapter five takes us through the bloody civil war of 1967 to 1970 during which an estimated three million people lost their lives. The civil war, as the this writer argues in the chapter, is the first indication of the crisis of the neocolonial state that was hurriedly put in place the by the departing British imperial power.

Chapter six depicts the intensification of state repression of political opponents in the face of a rapidly deteriorating national economy. Chapter seven examines the military's bogus agenda for transition to civil rule. The chapter also looks at the sorts of internal obstacles that continue to make the building of an enduring democratic structure an elusive task.

In chapter eight, the author examines the current opposition movement to the military government, and argue that the United Democratic Front of Nigeria's (UDFN) platform and program for transforming the Nigerian State into a democratic one are based on false premises, unnecessary compromises, and are most likely to fail. And finally, chapter nine rounds up the arguments developed in the previous chapters. It examines new possibilities for nation building and proposes a strategy for developing a more relevant political structure that would take into account the ethnic diversity of the Nigerian society. The chapter dismisses all the options that are being proposed by Nigerian politicians and intellectuals as solutions to the current crisis of economy, polity, and society in Nigeria.

Pade Badru

Chapter 1

Introduction:
The Geography and The People of Nigeria

In the more than three decades of political independence, many African states have gone through several violent civil wars generated by ethnic animosities and intolerance. These wars have resulted in a total collapse of the civil society and a fragile social order that is often accompanied by organized pogroms as was recently the case in Rwanda. Today, the political picture of many African nations is characterized by the disintegration of the political structure and a disorganized national economy incapable of providing subsistence for the masses of the people. One explanation for this may be found in the role ethnicity continues to play in the new emerging states, the majority of these artificial state entities were put together and defined by the selfishness of former colonial powers, especially France and Britain. The on going human disasters, including famine, genocide, and massacres of innocent civilians in Rwanda, Burundi and elsewhere in Africa, shows clearly the severity of the ethnic issue in black Africa. There is no other place where this ethnic time bomb is more frightening than Nigeria, which already has gone through a major civil war. This book is an attempt to understand the role ethnicity plays in nation building and its implication for the instability of the neocolonial state in the developing world and Nigeria in particular.

Nigeria is the most populous nation in sub-Saharan Africa with an estimated population of 100 million people of very diverse backgrounds. It is often said that one out of four black people on the face of the earth is a Nigerian. In terms of land mass, it is the second largest country in black Africa. The land mass spreads over a total area of 356,667 square miles, this is twice the size of California. The land area consists of disparate climate with the Sahara desert to the far north giving way to scrubland and savannah of the middle belt and the equatorial forests of the south. In the north, the country is bounded by the Afro-Arabic people of Niger and Chad; in east by the republic of the Cameron, which was a former territory of colonial Nigeria; and to the west, by the Benin Republic one of the few principalities of the Oyo kingdom and a primary source of slaves during the mid 16th and early 17th centuries.

Nigeria is made up of two hundred and fifty ethnic groups and thousands of different linguistic and dialect groups. The four dominant ethnic groups are the Fulanis and Hausa in the North, the Igbos in the southeast, and the Yoruba in the southwest. Each of these ethic groups is rich culturally and historically in a heritage and a distinctive character that separates one from the other. Indeed, the first known iron culture of any civilization was that of the Nok people of northern Nigeria. The Yoruba civilization was said to have spread northward in the direction of the upper Nile Valley, and westwards to the upper and lower Niger River valley ending somewhere in Timbuktu.

Table 1.1: Nigerian ethnic groups (1963)

Group	% of population
Hausa-Fulani	29.5
Kanuri	4.1
Tiv	2.5
Nupe	1.2
Yoruba	20.3
Edo	1.7
Ibo	16.6
Ibiobio	3.6
Ijaw	2.0
All others	17.5

Source: Etienne, V. *Who is Who and Where in Nigeria,* Africa Report, 1, January, 1970.

Within each of the principal ethnic groups, there are minigroups united by language, and whose minority status, continues to generate political discontent and nationalism which characterize the Nigerian political landscape. Indeed, the perception of ethnic domination by minority groups may help explain why the political landscape has been, and continues to be, susceptible to constant instability.

In terms of natural resources, the country is probably the richest in all of sub-Saharan Africa with vast deposits of crude petroleum, uranium, tin, gold, timber, and rubber. During colonial time the abundance of natural resources led to several clashes between the major colonial masters, especially the British, French, and Germans. In 1884, at the infamous partitioning of Africa at the Berlin conference, Nigeria came under the colonial influence of the British. Initially, the British exerted control over three protectorates, namely the northern, eastern, and Lagos protectorates. These were merely economic entities exploited primarily by the British crown for its own aggrandizement.

By 1914, in response to the constant violation of colonial boundaries by French bandits and outlaws, and also in response to increasing opposition to colonial exploitation by local chiefs, the British merged the three protectorates and declared a new nation that was to be known as Nigeria. Thus, the creation of Nigeria by the British imperial state was merely for administrative purposes. As far as geopolitics is concerned, Nigeria is simply an amalgam of different cultures with very little shared historical or socio- cultural characteristics. As Graf observes:

> Thus the territory of present Nigeria was defined, not on the basis of its peoples' shared historical, economic or social experiences, but merely by arbitrary amalgamation of a number of disparate ethnocultural units which happened to occupy contiguous land areas that were then under British colonial administration. Today, the ruthless, often brutal, methods of British conquest of Nigerian peoples, and the latter's prolonged resistance to it, are often forgotten or downplayed. (Graf, 1988; p.7)

For the one hundred years of British colonial rule, no attempt was made at creating a nation out of these several nationalities. Instead the British used ethnicity as a weapon to sustain its own rule. Thus it is not surprising that the nationalist elites that took over the state have very little idea of what the enormous task of nation building is all about. Instead of building a nation out of these diverse, and sometimes incompatible ethnic groups, the nationalist elites have found it convenient, as the British colonialists did, to maintain this divisiveness and, therefore, their hold on power.

Nationalism and Decolonization

Contrary to the popular belief held by scholars such as Ake (1980, 1981) that colonialism did not result in the transformation of the productive forces in a way that will result in the creation of social classes, evidence suggests that class formation progressed both during and before colonization. (Badru, 1993). In reality, colonial penetration of Nigerian society did lead to the formation of primordial classes and elites, especially in the export related agricultural activities and in mining where a significant working class had developed (Onimade, 1984). In the countryside, export crops production did give rise to a differentiation of rural peasantry (Badru,1993; p.188-193). At the time, the export- led economy also created African middlemen who continuously took advantage of trading between the European metropolitan business magnates and the African peasantry.

The majority of the middlemen were scattered around the costal regions of Lagos and the southeast. Similarly, in the hinterland, powerful Nigerian traders especially in the former north and eastern protectorates, emerged as big transport owners whose livelihood was also tied to export crops in cocoa, rubber, cotton, palm oil, palm kernels, and groundnuts. In the north, precolonial Hausa and Fulanis trading families also took advantage of colonial trading by moving their capital into new areas of business created by the new colonial economy (Bala, 1979). As a result of these trading activities, many powerful trading elites consolidated their economic positions under colonial rule, and the dominant strata of this group, were very influential in the years leading to political independence.

In the urban centers, particularly Lagos, Kano, Enugu, and Ibadan, colonial businesses provided the basis for the formation of the nascent Nigerian working classes. In Lagos, the majority of the working class were employed in the docks, while others were working for colonial trading houses such as the United African Company (UAC), Lever Brothers, Patterson and Zochonis (PZ), and numerous garment and light industries that were dominated by the Lebanese bourgeoisie and smaller foreign capital (Onimade 1980). The largest concentration of Nigerian wage workers were found in the mining industries, particularly coal mining in Enugu, and the tin and bauxite mines of Jos. Usually, rights to mining were given to European investors; however, a few members of the Nigerian trading class did get the right to engage in mining activities.

Despite the significant degree of class formation during colonial times, class consciousness and class based action amongst the peasantry and the working class were very mini-mal. In the cities, workers continued to identify with ethnic organizations which provided the social and economic sup-port needed for the peasants who had been uprooted from the countryside. Such organizations as Igbo Union and Egbe Omo Oduduwa were important primordial units that were used in integrating the newly arriving peasants from the countryside into the city milieu. The same ethnic organizations also pro-vided welfare provisions in the form of shelters and tempo-rary financial support for newly arriving peasants.

Because of the lack of proper infrastructure for recruit-ing workers into the colonial capitalist enterprises, these eth-nic organizations became the main recruiting agencies for the European-dominated economy. In effect, workers' allegiance on the factory floor was first and foremost, to those members of same ethnic group who had found them their jobs. The result of this personal contact at the level of production was that factory politics and competition were geared toward gain-ing ethnic advantage as opposed to class solidarity against the colonial exploiters. Ethnic solidarity, as opposed to class soli-darity, became the norm, thereby providing European entre-preneurs with a climate of obedience and ethnic rivalry which boosted productivity and lessened working class action on the factory floors and in the mines.

The Struggle for Independence

The nationalist struggle for independence was led by educated elites, who acquired their education in England or the United States, and by individuals who were self-taught, like the late Yoruba leader, Chief Obafemi Awolowo, who had previously worked in the colonial civil service. The constituencies of these nationalist leaders were the various ethnic organizations in the cities and the countryside. The fight for independence by these elites was nothing more than a fight for ethnic domi-nation. In the south, where the majority of the educated elites were concentrated, ethnic politics was promoted to a new level of banality.

In the former western protectorate, the Action Group (AG) was the party that represented the interests of the Yorubas, and in the east, the National Council of Nigerian Citizens (NCNC) was the exclusive preserve of the Igbos. The leadership of both these parties had very little support beyond their own ethnic groups except for Nmamidi Azikiwe who won elections in the west.

In the north, the political formation was slightly different. The Northern Peoples Congress (NPC) was clearly dominated by the northern feudal oligarchy. The leadership of the NPC was not particularly interested in early political independence for the country, fearing that political independence would only bring about the domination of the country by the educated southern elites. Instead, the northern leadership proposed a limited form of independent nationhood in which the political authority of the British would still be recognized. As an alternative, the northern leadership advocated a sort of regional independence that would have allowed any part of the nation to choose to become an independent sovereign state. The first option, as one would expect, was very agreeable to the British colonialists, because under their tutelage they could design a system that would ensure continuing domination by the imperial state. The alternative was not very suitable for British economic interest, because a disjointed Nigeria could spell trouble to British capital.

The Northern Peoples Congress's position on independence was very understandable. First, the northern business and political elites had economic interests that were tied to British rule. The fact that the British colonialists did not tamper with the rigid class system and the religious ideology that had sustained the feudalistic emirate system for so long, perhaps accounted for the northern leadership's objection to early independence.

The decision to grant independence to Nigeria, even though it was not to the imperial state's advantage, may have been influenced by several factors. One of these was the Mau Mau war in Kenya during the 1950s, which had claimed many European lives, and which had given British colonialism a bad name; it was not an event the British would have liked to see repeated in West Africa. The other reason that led the British to go to the negotiating table was the defeat of the French in North Africa which had claimed many French lives. And finally, the Enugu coal miners' revolts in the 1940s, and the Aba women's revolts that preceded it, convinced the British that the use of force was not going to work. In addition to all of these, the increasing militancy of the urban workers in support of the Enugu coal miners was of growing concern to the British, who were beginning to sense a buildup of a strong class solidarity among the urban workers.

By recognizing its own advantage, in the face of the factional competition within the various nationalist political parties, the British were able to impose a political arrangement that was to create the foundation for today's military intervention in the political process. In desperation, the British imperial state had succumbed to pressure from powerful northern economic interests and designed a constitution that gave serious concessions to northern elites. The parliamentary model that was proposed was modulated by a system of proportional representation in which the federal parliament would be dominated by the ethnic group with the largest population.

In addition to this, the new parliamentary system created the position of a prime minister who would wield executive power, and a figurehead president. This political model had its own inherent difficulty, which may explain why the first republic easily collapsed. This inherent contradiction was analyzed in a report submitted to the military government of General Olusegun Obasanjo, which was trying to figure out why the first republic failed despite positive expectations on the part of the British.

The report noted that:

> The separation of the Head of State from Head of Government involves a division between real authority and formal authority. The division is meaningless in the light of African political experience and history. The tendency among all people throughout the world is to elevate a single person (sic) to the position of a ruler.

In the context of Africa, the division is not only mean-
ingless, it is difficult to practice.... The system (British type parliamentary system) has resulted in a clash
of personalities and of interest, a conflict of authority
and unnecessary complexity and uncertainty in governmental relations. (Constitution drafting committee
report, vol 1, p.xxix, Lagos, 1976).

The southern leadership who objected to this arrangement were
threatened with exclusion from the decolonization negotia-
tion, and hence, postcolonial political process. For their personal aggrandizement, the leadership of the AG and the NCNC
went along with this arrangement hoping that in later years
the constitution might be amended to give full representation
to all. This was never to be the case. In fact ethnic minorities
who are outside of the three major ethnic groups of Hausa,
Yoruba, and Igbo fully represented in the first republic. Indeed by the time of the first military coups minority agitations
reached a point that threatened the stability of the union, and
it was in response to this that General Yakubu Gowon created
the first set of states out of the old regional arrangement.

Regional Self Rule

Attempts by organized labor unions to form an independent
working class based political party were undermined by pro-
hibitive labor laws, and by a naive nationalist elite, who perceived their political hegemony in the incoming independent
nation to be threatened by such a labor move. Thus, deep
seated class antagonisms were subsumed under ethnic ideologies. This was clearly demonstrated in the 1958 regional elections, which were supposed to prepare the nationalists for
eventual takeover of power after independence. Except for
the old western region, where Dr.Azikiwe's NCNC was voted
into power, assembly representations countrywide reflected
ethnic configurations.

In the northern assembly, ethnic Hausas and Fulanis, who
were faithful to their traditional leader the Sadauna of Sokoto,
Sir Ahmadu Bello, were overwhelmingly voted into power.

The same ethnic voting in the former eastern region saw that the followers of Dr.Azikiwe, later president of the first republic, controlled the regional assembly. The voting pattern in the regional elections gave an indication of the serious political instability that was to follow.

The first sign of trouble came in the form of complaints from ethnic minorities, most especially in the middle belt and riverine areas of southeastern Nigeria. The inability of the ethnic minorities to gain adequate representation soon gave rise to separatist movements that threatened the stability of the postcolonial state. This was temporarily resolved by the creation of additional subregions of middle belt and the Midwestern Nigeria. The second sign of trouble relates to several complaints of electoral frauds in the old western region which was encouraged by the resident British electoral officers in an effort to forestall the political ambitions of the Yoruba leader, Chief Obafemi Awolowo, whom the British suspected of being a communist.

Politically motivated riots and thuggery eventually led to the declaration of a state of emergency in the western region when the Action Group failed to win election to the federal assembly in 1961. However by 1963, ethnic solidarity in the western region had broken down when the Action Group was split into two irreconcilable factions the "progressives" and the "traditionalists". In the 1963 election, the Yoruba votes were split between the traditionalists led by Awolowo, and the renegade Chief Oladoke Akintola, the leader of the southern progressives, who had seen a vision of a united Nigeria in the form of consolidating the alliance between the North and South.

The political fallout in the old western region, between Akintola and Awolowo, eventually led to political compromises between the breakaway faction of the AG and the dominant northern NPC. In addition, the declaration of a state of emergency in the West, as a result of political violence and mayhem, was also followed by the suspension of self rule for the region. The old western region had, by then, provided the test case for the newly instituted political culture and the fragile union between the Muslim north and the Christian south.

Consequently, the irreconcilability of all these different levels of contradictions, cumulated in the military coup of 1966. On the national level, the federal assembly election was won by the NPC, a party that was favored by the British because of the political moderation of its leadership.

The northern elites' consolidation of their grip on the national government created ethnic animosities, and many southern members of the elites, by now, were openly calling for a form of confederacy. The Northerners' control of the federal government could only be a reality if it could control the repressive apparatus of the state. In the meantime, the military officer corps continued to be controlled by northern officers, and it is clear that they would use force to maintain control of the state.

In sum, this initial crisis reflects the inability of any strata of the emerging elite to exert total control over the neocolonial state. A number of reasons may account for this. First, the structural contradictions generated by the emerging political culture could not be absorbed enough to guarantee a stable political order. Second, the primacy assigned to the advancement of British economic interest, after political independence, produced a state that was susceptible to disintegration. And finally, the readiness of the nationalist elite to accept the unworkable constitution, imposed by the British imperial state, clearly laid the foundation for the future disintegration of the new state.

Chapter 2

State Theories and the Peripheral States: The Nigerian Case

The turbulent character of many Third World states has led social scientists to question the validity of existing state theories especially in the context of experiences of developing societies. In this chapter, therefore, state theories are evaluated with a view to establishing their relevance to our understanding of the peculiarity of the Nigerian state. The purpose of this is to reveal how weak- state structures in Nigeria gave way to the political and economic crises that have characterized the nation since its independence. In traditional social sciences, most theories of the state reflect their western extraction. Most of these theories take for granted the universal functions of the state as extracted from the particular form of states in western societies. The poverty of theories of peripheral states also reflects the Eurocentric bias in the social sciences. This chapter reviews existing theories of the state and their relevance to the analysis of the specificity of state forms in developing societies.

Classical Theory of the State

The conception of the state as a guarantor of citizenship and protector of individual rights is dominant in political and economic sciences. This approach derived from the philosophical tradition of Europe during the Enlightenment period. The works of Thomas Hobbes, John Locke, James Mill, Jeremy

Bentham, and John Stuart Mill represent the watershed of classical and liberal theories of the state. The common assumption shared by the classical theorists is that the state represents the general interests of all members of society. In other words, the state is a set of neutral institutions enforcing the rule of law without regard to socio-economic origins of all the members in a given social formation.

In this classical model, the legitimacy of the state to enforce rules and secure consensus is generally taken for granted. Different theories of the state put forward by the classical philosophers reflect their views on human nature. For Hobbes, human nature is "fixed" and "static"; human beings, by their very nature, are greedy, prone to violence, self centered, egoistical, and possessive. Given this set of human characteristics, a particular form of state is necessary to regulate human behavior so that society can avoid the self-centered rule of the powerful members of society, and protect the weaker members from the autocracy and tyranny of the few. Thus the state becomes, in the classical viewpoint, a natural institution as opposed to being the product of social relations between classes.

The political philosophy of Hobbes was put forward in his classic book, *Leviathan*, which was written at a time of intense economic transformation in Europe. Hobbes was very much concerned, above all, with the problems of order in a new economic system that was later to be known as capitalism. Although writing at a time when absolutism was the order of the day, his work envisioned the emergence of a new system of production in which competition for influence and political power, between the emerging mercantile class and the feudal oligarchy, might impinge upon or undermine the stability of the absolutist state.

In *Leviathan*, Hobbes explored the relationship between human nature, society and the state. Humans always pursue, what Hobbes called "good", and further more, humans always have "appetites" and "desires" (Hobbes, 1969; p.120). The ability of humans to satisfy appetites and desires is what Hobbes called power, which is necessary for the maintenance of human material existence as in continuous motion. In as much as power is the means to attaining Good, it becomes the preoccupation of human endeavor. This conceptualization of power in human conditions necessarily led Hobbes to the formulation of his theory of state thus:

> So that in the first place, I put for general inclination of all mankind, a perpetual and restless desire of power after power, that ceaseeth only in death. And the cause of this not always that a man hopes for a more intensive delight, than he had already attained to, or that he cannot assure the power and the means to live well, which he hath at present, without the acquisition of more. (Hobbes,1968;p.161)

The human condition is such that it is in ceaseless motion in the pursuit of power to satisfy the desire for material good. This process then produces in human beings, a reckless need for aggression, selfishness, and a ruthlessness that accompanies the pursuit of power. The search for pleasure and self aggrandizement necessarily leads to quarrelling among humans; quarrelling causes the instability of the social order. Hobbes identified three principal sources of quarrel among humans: these are competition, difference, and glory. This condition, according to Hobbes, is incompatible with human development, and the survival of the human race:

> Whatsoever is consequent to the time of Warre (sic.), where every man is enemy to every man, the same is consequent to the time, wherein men live without security, than what their own strength, and their own invention shall furnish them withal. In such condition, there is no place for industry; because the fruit thereof is uncertain: and consequently no Culture of the earth: no navigation, nor the use of the commodities that may be imported by Sea; no commodious building, nor instruments of moving, and removing such things as require much force; no Knowledge of the face of the Earth; no account of Time, no Arts, no Letters; no Society; and which is worst of all, continual fear, and

danger of violent death; And the life of man, poor,
nasty, brutish and short. (Hobbes,1968,p.185)

The picture of humans in a state of war as described by Hobbes
meant that there could be no justice, injustice, right, or wrong.
Hobbes proposed an absolutist state, in which monarchy is
the only solution for rescuing human society from the chaos
and lawlessness that pursuit of self-happiness and crude pas-
sions often generate. The state, in the Hobbesian model, derived from the principle of natural laws, and the notion of
social contract emerged by which individuals gave up certain
rights of "self government".

The sovereign thus becomes the legitimate guardian of
individual rights and exercises legitimate power over its subjects. In Hobbes's formulation, the sovereign could be an individual, such as a monarch, or a collective body, like an assembly. In the first instance, the sovereign monopolizes power
and can not be limited in its authority by any existing power
block. Finally, a good sovereign is judged by its impartiality
and its ability to ensure contracts among its subjects, to enforce agreements and to protect the rights of weak from the
powerful. Hobbes was strongly in favor of an absolute monarchy because according to him:

> It follows that where the public and private interests
> are most closely united, there is the public most ad-
> vanced. Now in the Monarchy, the private interest is
> the same with the public. The riches, power, and honor
> of a monarch arise only from the riches, strength and
> reputation of his Subjects. For no King can be rich,
> nor glorious, nor secure; whose Subjects are either
> poor, or contemptible, or too weak through want, or
> dissention, to maintain war against their enemies.
> (Hobbes, 1968; p.241-242)

In essence, the sovereign or state, in Hobbes' work, is the
absolute precondition for human development; without the
state, human progress is impossible. However it is obvious
that at the time Hobbes was writing, the industrial revolution

was in the offing. Clearly, the development of capitalism requires the expansion of the market, and active state intervention and regulation were absolutely necessary, if the emerging system of capitalist production was to be firmly implanted. The triumph of mercantilism over feudalism, and later, of industrial capitalism over mercantilism, meant a reassessment of the idea of an absolute monarchy that was proposed in Hobbes's works.

Another classical theorist of note is John Locke (1632-1704), whose work paved the way for the idea of western democracy as we know it today. Like Hobbes, Locke extracted his theory of state from the principles of human nature outlined in Hobbes work, *Leviathan*. However, the similarities end there. Unlike Hobbes, humans in "the state of nature" were not as ruthless as Hobbes would have us to believe. Indeed, humans enjoy life, health, liberty, possessions; all these are God given. The implication of Locke's proposition is the undermining of Hobbes's emphasis on the monarchy as the provider of liberty. The "state of war", which Hobbes used in characterizing the state of nature (anarchy), was now replaced by the laws of nature which, according to Locke, guided human actions.

Locke's idea of humans in a state of nature, in harmony with each other, presupposes a recognition of the freedom with which humans are naturally endowed, or what is referred to in modern times as inalienable rights. For Locke:

> To understand political power and rights...., we must consider what state all men are naturally in , and that is a state of perfect freedom to order their actions and to dispose of their possessions and persons as they think fit, within the bounds of the laws of nature, without asking leave or depending on the will of any other man. (Locke, 1952; p.4)

However this freedom may be undermined by individuals taking the laws into their own hands. Consequently, "a state of war" exists only when the rights of an individual are violated by force or threat of force in the absence of a common superior.' The idea of a common superior was later to form the cornerstone of Locke's theory of the state. Locke proposed a republican state.

Whereas, Hobbes discountenanced private poverty, Locke saw private property as the fundamental basis of the state. One of the fundamental rights of human beings is their ability to accumulate possessions to meet their most basic needs. If the state of nature resembles anything like war as Hobbes suggests, it is only because the rights of individuals to accumulate possessions are violated by force or threat of war.

> The state of nature has a law of nature to govern it, which obliges everyone; and reason, which is that law teaches all mankind who will but consult that, being all equal and independent, no one ought harm another in his life, health, liberty or possessions. (Locke,1952, p.5).

Since unguarded freedom may ultimately undermine the stability of the social order, and by inference, of individual rights, Locke returns to the theme of "common superior power", which is synonymous to a "community of wills". In this regard, individuals give up their rights and natural power to "the community of wills" which becomes the recognized umpire by setting up rules which are indifferent and uniformly applied to all parties. The common superior that is, " the common wills", thus becomes the entity that protects the rights of private poverty, life, liberty and estate, against the injuries of other men. This legislative power, which Locke was later to call the "common superior power", cannot be invested in a single person as Hobbes suggested, but in a legislative body selected from people of property. This is in sharp contrast to Hobbes's idea of absolute monarchy.

The point here is that, Locke's idea, which was latter pursued in the works of James Mill and John Stuart Mill, and other modern day liberal philosophers, formed the theoretical basis of contemporary liberal democratic ideas of the capitalist state. However, the idea of a liberal democratic model proposed in the works of these later writers is qualitatively different than that proposed by Locke. As Sabine observes:

> Benthan, Mill and Utilitarians generally provided one of the clearest justifications for the liberal democratic state which ensures the conditions necessary for individuals to pursue their interests without risk of arbitrary political interference, to participate freely in economic transactions, to exchange labor and goods on the market and to appropriate resources privately."
> (Sabine, 1961, pg.16)

The role of property in political participation, in Locke's work, delimits the scope of participation in the legislative process, since only those individuals with property could qualify. However latter day liberal democratic theorists no longer see property as the basis for political participation. As a result of this, they see the capitalist state as an impartial state representing the interests of all in the civil society. The neutrality of the state proposed in these earlier theories have come under severe attack in the works of western Marxists to which we now turn.

Critique of the Liberal Democratic State

There is no systematic theory of the capitalist state in the collaborative works of Marx and Engels, the founding fathers of radical critique in the social sciences. The absence of state theory in their work may be due to the fact that their focus was mostly on the class structure of capitalism as a system of production and the revolutionary possibilities within it. The first outline of a Marxian theory of the state could be traced to the work of the, Vladimir Lenin. Following Marx's sketches in the *Communist Manifesto*, Lenin saw the capitalist state as nothing more than an instrument of the ruling class; an instrument used to enforce its political and economic agendas on the rest of civil society. The liberal parliament was seen by Lenin as an executive arm of the bourgeois state serving bourgeois interests. It was much later that Marxist scholars began to examine the relation of the capitalist state to the dominant classes, and the medium through which bourgeois interests are realized by the state.

In his very controversial book, *The State in Capitalist Society*, Ralph Miliband dismisses the liberal notion of the democratic state in which the interests of all social classes are realized and safe guarded. The capitalist state, according to Miliband, could only serve the interest of the capitalist class. In a study of the various institutions of the state, namely the parliament, big business, educational institutions, mass media, and the military, Miliband discovers that the ruling elites in all of these bourgeois institutions 1). have identical class background and social connections; 2). attended the same elite schools and belonged to the same social clubs and business circles. As a result of this common class background, the ruling elites, Milliband contends, must by simple logic pursue policies that advance the economic interests, and the political agenda of their privileged class:

> The evidence conclusively suggests that in terms of social origin, education, and class situation, the men who have manned all command positions have been largely, in many cases, overwhelmingly, drawn from the world business and property, or from the professional middle class. (Miliband, 1973; p.61).

The conclusion drawn in Miliband's book is that contemporary capitalist formations are characterized by "plurality of elites" (e.g. political elites made up of the parliament, the corporate oligarchies, the military elites, and the petty state officials). These elites, in their private and public life, pursue policies that enhance capitalist profit which is essential to class domination.

Nicos Poulantzas, another Marxist, has objected strongly to Miliband's response to the liberal theory of the state. In particular, Poulantzas objects to Miliband's notion of the "plurality of elite", which according to him, was imported into Miliband's critique of the thesis of the "managerial elitism". Poulantzas rebuked Miliband for remaining essentially within the domain of "bourgeois empiricism" by attempting to use empirical data to demonstrate the existence of the ruling class:

> Miliband considers managers as one among the distinct economic elites...... I consider this a mistaking way of presenting the problem. To start with, the distinct criterion for membership of the capitalist class is no way a motivation of conduct, that is to say, the search for profit as the 'aim of action'......Marx criterion is the objective place in production and the ownership of the means of production. (Poulantzas, 1973; p.243).

In Poulantzas's view, motivation for profit cannot be the sole defining characteristic of a capitalist. Such a definition, according to Poulantzas, will reduce the essential contradiction of the capitalist mode of production to one between its social character and its private appropriation, that is, motivation for profit. For Poulantzas, the real contradiction is between the socialization of the productive forces and the private appropriation of surplus produce. The implication of Poulantzas's argument thus far is that managers do not constitute distinct stratum of the capitalist class, nor for that matter, a distinct economic elite.

On the question of the relationship of the various elites in state institutions to the bourgeoisie, Poulantzas argues that Miliband only trivialized the problematic by reducing elite control of the bourgeois state to personal ties. For Poulantzas, understanding the relationship between the state and the capitalist class is an objective one. In other words, this relation is not reducible to personal ties or to some sort of psychologism (conduct of social actors) as Miliband suggests. For Poulantzas, understanding the objective relation between the bourgeois class and the state requires, first and foremost, the understanding of the objective function of the capitalist state. The capitalist state functions to reproduce the relations of exploitation; a necessary precondition for reproducing the social formation:

> The relation between the bourgeois class and the State
> is an objective relation. This means that if the function
> of the state in a determinate social formation and the
> interests of the dominant classes in this formation co-
> incide, it is by the reason of the system itself: the di-
> rect participation of the members of the ruling class in
> the State apparatus is not the cause but the effect, and
> moreover a chance and contingent one, of this objec-
> tive coincidence. (Poulantzas, 1969; p.73)

In *Political Power and Social Classes*, Poulantzas outlines, in great detail, the function of the capitalist state and shows how state structures function to reproduce elite domination. Following the French structural functionalist tradition of Louis Althusser and Etiene Balibar, Poulantzas sees the function of the state in a determinate social formation and the interest of the dominant class as naturally coinciding. The primary function of the state, Poulantzas argues, is to promote the unity of the social formation. This unity consists of, among other things, ensuring a conducive climate under which expanded reproduction and capital accumulation are made possible. This entails the state enforcing the social and political hegemony of the class of the owners of capital, which means that the state must promote ideology that legitimizes the process of expropriation of surplus labor.

However, Poulantzas notes that the system of capitalist expropriation (veiled by the apparent legality of existing wage relations and the cultural emphasis on work ethics among lower classes) is ridden with antagonistic contradictions that directly threaten the unity of the social formation. The state must, therefore, assume a posture of neutrality in order to be able to resolve these contradictions. The state is thus capable of intervening, because of its apparent neutrality, in the struggle between labor and capital over the distribution of surplus produce. Unlike Miliband, Poulantzas believed that the state performs this function well only when the members of the capitalist class do not participate directly in the apparatus of the state.

The Miliband-Poulantzas debate generated an intense interest within a wide spectrum of scholars including liberals and Marxists alike. The central objection to the neo-Marxists' instrumentalist and structuralist conception of the states centers around the question of human agency. In order words, what role do individual social actors play in shaping the policy of the state? The other objection relates to the issue of the autonomy of the state with regard to social classes.

In Fred Block's book (1977), *The Origins of the International Economic Disorder*, he raises issue with a particular brand of Marxist state theory that reduces the state to a tool in the hands of the ruling class. This instrumentalist conception of the state, according to Block, underestimates the role of the state as a legitimizer of the social order. In performing the role of a legitimizer, Block argues, the capitalist state must invoke an appearance of neutrality, and for the state to effectively advance the general interest of the capitalist class, it must disconnect itself from the most powerful strata of the bourgeoisie. In essence, the apparent neutrality of the capitalist state, in enforcing social relations between labor and capital, is a precondition for bourgeois class domination that characterizes western democracies that have been so well written about. According to Block:

> ... instrumentalist fails to recognize that to act in the interest of capital, the state must be able to take action against particular interest of capitalists. Price control or restriction on export of capital, for example, might be in the general interest of capital at this particular period even if they temporarily reduced the profits of most capitalists. To carry through such policies, the state must have autonomy from direct capitalist control than the instrumentalist view would allow. (Block,.1977; p.9)

What needs specifying, Block continues, is the limit of this relative autonomy of the state that most Marxist theorists have failed to define.

Since the famous Poulantzas and Miliband debate, other neo-Marxist scholars have contributed towards a Marxist theory of the state. Unfortunately, most of the literature on the capitalist state is either instrumentalist or structuralist in its approach. Most notable is that of the German derivationist school (Claus Offe, Bernard Blanke, Hans Kanstendiek). While these neo-Marxist scholars have avoided a structuralist explanation, they ended up, like Polantzas, by either seeing state functions as deriving from the "logic of capital", or as serving the needs and reproduction of capital. These neo-Marxists ended up presents a theory of the state that makes the state and its functions impossible to empirically verify.

In an attempt to bridge the gap between voluntarism and structuralism in neo-Marxists theories of the state, William G. Domhoff, proposes a state theory that combines an analysis of agency and structure. In *The Powers That Be* and *Who Rules America?*, Domhoff explores the relationship between the hegemonic block of the ruling class and the capitalist state. Domhoff concludes that the ruling class dominates the state by its over representation in both corporate bodies and governmental institutions. The ruling class, according to Domhoff, exercises its influence over state institutions through several processes such as lobbying, special interest, candidate selection, ideology and so forth. But he fails to show how the ruling class comes to dominate these processes, and through what mechanisms the ruling class interests are served by state policies.

Part of the of the answer to this question has been provided by Block. According to Block, the capitalist state relies on investment to generate the economic activities upon which state's income is dependent. The capitalist class, Block continues, can use this dependence as a "veto" on state officials in order to promote policies that would advance the general interest of capital:

> In capitalist economy, the level of economic activities are largely determined by the private investment decisions of the capitalists. That means that capitalists, in their collective role as investors, have a veto over state

> policies in that their failure to invest at adequate levels
> can create major political problems for state manag-
> ers. This discourage state managers from taking ac-
> tions that might seriously decrease the rate of invest-
> ment. It also means that managers in using their power
> to facilitate investment, since their continued power
> rests on a healthy economy. (Block,1977; p.15)

The implication of Block's argument is that state managers
are nothing more than tools in the hands of the capitalist class,
since the capitalist class can use investment decisions to dictate state policies. This is precisely the same instrumentalist
position which Block sets himself against.

Block found himself in a situation similar to that of the
instrumentalist theorists because of his inability to formulate a
coherent theory of the "relative autonomy" of the state that
did not derive from the economic structure. The failure of
Marxist scholars to separate analysis at the level of the theoretical from the political often results in deterministic models
which Marxism had been struggling to break away from. However, Block deserves credit for focusing our attention on how
capitalist accumulation and investment decisions influence state
policies; policies that are geared toward advancing the general interest of the capitalist class.

Since this is not the appropriate place to elaborate on the
different tendencies within Marxist historiography, what is of
interest to this author here is: how can we understand the
specificity of the state in the periphery of the world economy,
using some of the categories derived from the analysis of the
capitalist state in western democracies. The problems of political instability, as I argue here, we cannot be divorced from
the contradictions embedded in neo-colonial state formation
in the periphery especially black Africa. The concluding section of this chapter looks at state form in the third world and
its relation to both internal, and external social classes.

The Neocolonial state

As noted above, most of the existing theories of the state in the social sciences, have, as their focus, state forms in contemporary capitalist formations. The result is that an analysis of state forms (and their functions) in the Third World often uses categories that were derived from an analysis of state in advanced industrial western societies. However, with the debate between Miliband and Poulantzas generating new concepts such as the "relative autonomy" of the state, Third World scholars have begun to look at the specificity of the states in the periphery of the world economy.

In his well informed paper, "The Postcolonial State", Hamza Alavi (1978) was among the first wave of third world scholars to address the question of the usefulness of the relative "autonomy" of the state when analyzing state forms in the periphery. According to Alavi, the colonial state emerged to reflect the economic interests of social classes in the colonizing nation; as a result, its political economy is qualitatively different from states in the metropolitan centers of the world economy.

The underdevelopment of social classes in the periphery, according to Hamza Alavi, means that no single social group is capable of exerting its influence on the state. The postcolonial state, because of its historical specificity, acts in the first instance to advance the economic interests of metropolitan capital, and second, to regulate intra-class competition within internal hegemonic classes. Thirdly, it provides the conditions under which the process of accumulation is facilitated. By so doing, the neocolonial states reproduce and perpetuate colonial structures which results in constant instability of the state and the prevention of the development of an enduring political culture.

The essence of Alavi's argument is that the postcolonial state is independent of internal social classes but responds to external interest. The problem with this assertion is that metropolitan capital usually operates in alliance with a local ally, most especially, members of the comprador bourgeoisie. With the era of political independence, the economic power of the comprador bourgeoisie grew tremendously compared to that of other social classes. This economic power also brought enormous political power to the extent that members of the comprador bourgeoisie dominate directly or indirectly state structure through an elaborate system of clientelism (Turner, 1975; Turner and Badru, 1985).

The only challenge to the power of the comprador bourgeoisie usually comes from the national bourgeoisie whose vision of a truly bourgeois society is impeded by the alliance between metropolitan and internal comprador capital. As the author hopes to show, the friction between national and comprador capital often results in the instability of the state. The instability of the neocolonial state allowed for the continuing link with metropolitan capital and the underdevelopment of national bourgeoisie, which might lead the state on the path of independent national development.

In *Revolutionary Pressure in Africa*, Claude Ake (1978) argues that the underdevelopment of social classes in Africa may explain the absence of a class struggle. Class struggle, according to Ake, has the potential for transforming the polity and economy, and consequently of setting in motion revolutionary pressures for change. Ake is, perhaps, underestimating the extent to which colonial capital had created classes and their revolutionary potential. What needed to be explained is: Why have class conflicts and antagonisms failed to transform themselves at the level of the neo-colonial state? And why has the neo-colonial state failed to create the condition for the emergence of a progressive national bourgeoisie that would pursue the historic mission of its European counterpart? These are issues the following chapters hope to elucidate.

The Peculiarity of the Nigerian State

In the proceeding chapter we suggested that the transformation of the colonial state in Nigeria was essentially mediated through ethnicity. The complex pattern of antagonistic relationships within the class of the nationalist elite that fought for independence is intersected by class and ethnicity. The majority of the nationalists who were at the forefront of the struggle for independence were themselves representatives of hidden social classes who, because of some traditional or religious reasons, did not partake directly in the struggle for the control of the colonial state. In essence we have, after independence, at least on the surface, a state structure that reflected the economic interests of the feudal oligarchy, particularly from the North and the Lagos based comprador elite. The defining characteristic of the neocolonial state shortly after independence was the struggle between the feudal and the comprador elite in terms of the sort of alliance each would form with metropolitan capital.

Shortly before the civil war, and prior to the dominance of petroleum capital in national production, the feudal elite managed temporarily to exercise a certain degree of control over the neocolonial state. State policies and finances were determined by responses of production of export crops, and the unpredictable fluctuations in the world commodity market. Essentially, the productive sectors of the economy, which was largely controlled by British capital through such companies as Lever Brothers and the United African Company (UAC) remained clearly outside of the control of the new state. The Nigerian state at this time restricted its activities to collecting duties at borders and taxes from foreign companies to finance the operations of the state.

The relationship of the political elite to the federal state thus became the most important determining factor in political power; and the ability of the political elite to use such power to appropriate surplus in the form of taxes for regional development, depended largely on the sort of relationship they can establish with the neo-colonial state at the federal level. In fact, one can argue that the national state (that the state at the federal level) is of very little consequence to internal politics because the state itself continues to serve the interest of metropolitan capital.

At the regional level, state autonomy meant that the political elite could control state structures to accumulate capital, which was used for running elite pet programs. This was the case with the free universal education platform of the Action Group in the old western region. Usually, state marketing boards provide the arena for politics. As Helleiner (1966) suggests, the marketing boards were used by the nationalist elites to expropriate peasants' surplus labor. The crisis over the control of the regional states shortly after independence clearly laid the foundation for the political turmoils and military interventions that followed. In the context of the new Nigeria then, we have several states within a state.

The federal state can be said to be devoid of local elite control precisely because of the economic dominance of metropolitan capital. The crisis that engulfed the federation after 1964 reflects a poor articulation between the autonomy of regional states vis a vis the federal state. It was not until after the end of the civil war in 1970 that the relationship between regional authorities and the central state became more defined. Indeed, the war itself provided the medium for creating what is now known as the Nigerian state.

By the time the war ended, the alignment of class forces at the federal level had also changed. The creation of smaller state units from the old regions was followed by the loss of autonomy previously enjoyed by the regional authorities. As we mentioned elsewhere, the war itself marked the beginning of the end of the political power of the traditional feudal oligarchy and the rise of new social classes who now competed for control of the state at the federal level.

One of the most important developments after the war was the rise new social classes. The most stable and powerful of these were the state bureaucrats, the comprador elements of the national bourgeoisie, and the gentlemen soldiers who later became capitalist farmers. The relationship of each of these elites to international capital depended essentially on their current location within the system of production. The most visibly situated of the elites was the state bureaucratic elite who took the advantage of the rentier character of the state to position itself in the most strategic sector of the economic hierarchy. The state bureaucrats, especially the high-up technocrats, became the conduit for linking internal social elites to metropolitan capital (Turner, 1975).

Because of its administrative link to the military class, who by now controlled most state structures, the technocrats could determine which strata of the bourgeoisie received the favor of conducting business with international capital and at what cost. Clearly in this arrangement, the economic was subordinate to the political, which made the Marxist's instrumentalist conception of the state a mere absurdity. What we have in the Nigerian case is a constantly changing relationship between the elites at the level of politics and at the level of the economics. The relationship thus becomes a symbiotic one because neither the political nor the economic elite can do without the other in terms of its different relationship to metropolitan capital. In a sense, the Nigerian state thus projects an image of relative autonomy in its dealings with both international capital on the one hand and internal social classes on the other. But in actual fact, because of its neocolonial character, the Nigerian state is nothing more than a balancing apparatus, which ultimately must bow to the wishes of international capital.

In conclusion, one could argue that the peculiarity of the neocolonial state is characterized by both the changing nature of the arena of production and the demands of internal and external social classes. Given its balancing role, the peripheral state appears to remove itself from internal social forces so that it could pretend to represent the interest of all. In fact, the neocolonial state is so week to the point that it could hardly provide the necessary conditions for the sort of stability that is necessary to accommodate the explosive contradictions that are embedded in a peculiar situation of dependence that characterized late capitalist development in the periphery of the world economy.

One point that needed to be stressed is that, international capital's pretension for democratization, in the periphery, is nothing more than a facile pretension, because democratization at the periphery could only undermine the process of global capital accumulation. This is because, a neocolonial state could only function within the limits of the competition between internal social classes and international capital. In the last resort, a week neocolonial state, like the Nigerian state, would bow to the wishes of international capital instead of protecting the interests of internal social classes.

Chapter 3

Imperialism and Underdevelopment in Nigeria

The endemic problem of African economic crises has been analyzed by western liberal social sciences from a perspective that is generally Eurocentric. Western social sciences usually pose the question of African crises outside of the context of Africa's historical experience of colonial domination and the continuing imperialistic relations between African social formations and their formal colonial masters. Liberal economics, in particular, sees African economic crises as symptomatic of a social malaise that marks Africa off from the rest of the so-called civilized world. In this chapter, we therefore examine traditional theories of development with the view to assessing their relevance to the specific African experience.

Modernization School and African Development

The most dominant perspective in the study of social change is the modernization school of thought. Many modernization theorists see the problems of transformation as intricately linked to the rigidity of the traditional social structure of the developing societies (Einsenstadt 1965, 1966; Hokowitz, 1988). Eisenstadt argues that internal obstacles imposed by the rigidity of traditional structure contribute to the lack of transformation in many traditional societies. Shmuel Eisenstadt focuses, especially, on the hierarchy of traditional authority which, according to him, emphasizes gerontocratic power in all aspects of social and economic life. Eisenstadt further suggests that the lack of modernizing elites within this rigid social structure may explain why many developing societies have failed to achieve economic development.

In Eisenstadt's work, political modernization is often seen as a prelude to the process of economic development, and by inference, the historical path taken by Western societies is similarly proposed as the necessary path towards the evolution of structures that would allow for social and economic transformation (Hokowitz, 1988, Moore;1994). As Horton (1993) argues, political modernization must, above all, entail intellectual transformation, since traditional systems of thoughts are not compatible with the requirement of a modern economy (Horton, 1967, 1993).

This "tradition/modernity" approach has its roots in both western metaphysics and in Weberian analysis of the transition to western industrialism. Modernity, or the transition to industrialism, is characterized by the rationalization of the economic, political, and cultural structures of a given society. This transformation is necessary in order to achieve the type of efficiency upon which modern industrialism can be built (Abrams,1989:73-107). Using these as indices for measuring development, modernization scholars sees the European historical trajectory as a gauge for defining development.

Theoretically, the "traditional perspective'" approach may contain some useful points only if one is looking at the system of international economic development or global social change in a vacuum. This metaphysical viewpoint, which continues to dominate development discourse, summarizes clearly what is wrong with western interpretation of realities in the developing world. In short, it calls into question whether western social sciences, such as sociology and economics, have really understood the meaning of development. By defining social change in terms of the European historical trajectory, scholars like Eisenstadt and Hokowitz, not only foreclose the possibility of different path of historical transition but also deny the specificity of conditions in all human societies.

The "tradition/modernity" perspective did not begin with Eisenstadt, but represents the culmination of a long line of platitudinous analyses that continue to characterize post-World War II economic analyses of developing societies. The neo-classical Rostowrian perspective, which provided the intellectual and ideological basis for the post-war capitalist development model for developing societies, has confused our understanding of development in non-western societies. The refusal of many sociologists and development specialists to recognize the fact that Western imperialism has complicated, and continues to complicate Third World development experience, calls into question the utility of this traditional approach in sociology. Eisenstadt's analysis has further contributed to the lack of theoretical clarity in development discourse. This discourse is often predicated upon some ontological notions of human nature and history.

In Rostow's work (1968), there was a more coherent modernization theory that relied exclusively on positivistic and metaphysical interpretation of development. In the Rostowrian model, development is like to a copy cat game in which the developing world simply adopts fiscal policies that have enabled the Western societies to develop. In this neo-classical schema, development is measured as a percentage or ratio of investable savings to consumption. In the end, growth is defined purely in quantitative term, especially by the Gross National Produce (GNP). The modernization idea of development, as exemplified by Rostow, erroneously assumed equity and progress in the growth of the capitalist economy and, as result, ignores the painful realities of income distribution, the monopoly of resources by dominant classes, and the export oriented nature of production that limits economic growth in most developing societies.

By believing in the metaphysics of the free-market economy, the modernization school of thought calls for international capital's participation in Third World development. According to Rostow, countries that are lacking in development resources could open their doors to multinational corporations, the so-called agents of change, and with the right political climate, such countries could be on the road to a self sustaining development. Available evidence suggests the opposite (cf Susan George, 1992). Indeed, the current International Monetary Fund's (IMF) proposal for economic recovery in most of the developing world is based on this neoclassical idea. In fact, the past decade had witnessed many desperate African nations executing structural adjustment programs (SAP) that promised a quick economic fix.

In his seminal paper, Hokowitz (1988), introduces new absurdities to the modernization theory by classifying societies in terms of how closely they resemble the western model of development. In his latest article "Three Worlds Plus One," Hokowitz is at odds with himself in stressing that despite the modernization dreams of progress in the periphery of the world economy, the global economy is still basically divided between the rich North and the poor South. The industrialized countries of the North, according to Hokowitz, continue to prosper and enjoy breakthroughs in science and technology while the nations of the South sink deeper into poverty. But Hokowitz is unable to explain the dynamics that are responsible for the persistence of this dichotomy within the world system. Like Horton's, Hokowitz's metaphysics clearly demonstrates the type of arrogance that often characterizes western scholars' analysis of the problems of African development experience. The ahistorical nature of Hokowitz's reasoning brings up the question of whether modernization theorists have an agenda separate from their scholarly pursuits.

After fifty years of faithful commitment to the modernization paradigm, economic conditions in most developing nations, including those in the communist block, have deteriorated sharply. But despite the glaring failure of the neoclassical model, the developed industrial countries continue to promote this model in the developing world. The question then must be, which economic interest benefits from the continuing advocacy of this paradigm in Third World development? Indeed, many developing nations are yet to see tangible results of years of participation in the global economy. Which brings us, further, to the question of dependency in the world system.

Dependency in the World System

The failure of the modernization model in promoting sustained economic development in the Third World had led to the development of an alternative paradigm often dubbed as the "radical" or "conflict" perspective in development circle. This paradigm ranges from the simplistic dependency model to the more sophisticated world system theory. Unfortunately, this radical approach within sociology and political economy has ended up with the same problems that marred the modernization theories of development. Essentially, by sharing the same basic metaphysical belief in the possibility of a late capitalist development in the periphery of the world economy, the radical school went the same road as their modernization counterpart. This is not to suggest that what the radical school has to say has no explanatory value.

The radical scholars reminded us of the ahistorical character of the modernization theory. They sought explanation of underdevelopment in the very logic of capitalist development. Andre Gunder Frank (1965, 1970), one of the early popularizers of the dependency theory, blamed capitalist development in the metropolis for causing underdevelopment in the periphery. True enough, but how? Frank's main arguments rest mainly on the role that colonialism played in the early development of European capitalism. Colonialism, the argument goes, provided the initial accumulation for capitalist development, which at the same time created the very conditions for Third World underdevelopment. These conditions include among others, 1.) the drainage of potential investable resources from the periphery to the European metropolis through unequal exchange, 2.) the creation of a particular form of world division of labor that assigns subordinate and dependent roles to former European colonies (the periphery of the world economy), and 3.) the dominance of development ideology that locks in bureaucrats in the developing world into believing in the fairness of the current global political and economic arrangements (Amin, 1974; 1976, Wallerstein 1986; Stavenhagen, 1973).

Thus, for dependency scholars, peripheral formations can achieve sustained and autonomous economic growth only by breaking away from the suffocating world economic order. Breaking away from the international economic order, according to the dependency school, would require a socialist revolution. But Frank and the other radical scholars were hardly able to prescribe how this would be achieved given the current reality that the international economic order represents. In Frank's work, as in Rostow, Lerner, and Eisenstadt's, we have a new ideology, or religion of development, one that pays very little attention to the internal contradictions and capability of the developing societies. In fact, these radical development theories have very little vision of economic development that would be qualitatively different from the Western European experience. In a sense, we are made to believe is that the answer to the developing world's problems can come from this sort of analysis that does not take into consideration the realities or the perspectives of the poor men and women in the poorest section of the global economy.

Immanuel Wallerstein (1974) transformed dependency into a more coherent thesis in which the capitalist world system incorporates both the developed and the developing world with shared characteristics of development and underdevelopment. Unlike the dependency theory, underdevelopment, in this world system paradigm, is not a function of the capitalist development process but is indeed, an essential aspect of global capitalist accumulation, incorporating specific forms of division of labor that distinguish the center from the periphery.

In its broader argument, the world system theory sees development as a temporary advantage. World system theories argue that, within the current global capitalist system, the developed western metropolis has a temporary advantage, and with the possibility of a shift, the developed section of the world economy may occupy the subordinate position that is currently being occupied by the peripheral nations. What a relief! This dynamic equilibrium model draws its theoretical strength from the thesis of permanent and uneven development that comes from the work of Leon Trosky, especially his thesis on "permanent revolution" (cf McIntyre, 1993). However, it should be pointed that the world system theory differs significantly from the dependency theory in its dogmatic belief in world revolution that would shift the balance of power from the center to the periphery.

The political climate of the 1960s may have given inspiration to the ideas of a global revolution. However, there was hardly any clear indication that the system of capitalist expropriation was under any threat from internal social classes in the metropolis. Except for challenges that were posed by decolonization and the civil rights movement in the United States, increasing poverty in the periphery was accompanied by increased accumulation in the metropolitan centers of global capitalist production. Indeed, there was never a material basis for global working class unity that could generate the type revolution envisaged by the dependency and world system theorists.

Paul Baran's (1956) critique of the neo-classical perspective may have also inspired several radical researches in the late 1960s and 1970s. In particular, younger economists at the Economic Commission for Latin America (ECLA) like Cardoso (1972), Furtado (1970), and Dos Santos (1973), began to apply the political economy and dependency models to the understanding of the structures of underdevelopment in the Third World. Unlike the modernization theorists, these scholars saw underdevelopment not as a stage in the process of economic development, but as a peculiar condition brought about by capitalism's incursion into Third World economies. They emphasized the overdependency of Third World economies on the western metropolis, which continues to dictate the internal dynamics of the former. Colonialism, these authors argue, was a precursor to this peculiar situation of dependence (Frank, 1966).

Emmanuel Arghiri (1972) identifies the problem as one of unequal exchange between the periphery of the world economy and the Western metropolis. He argues that, unequal exchange between the underdeveloped countries and the Western nations arose out of "the maintenance of depressed wage rates and the use of monopoly power by industrial nations to turn the terms of trade against the Third World " (Eicher, 1990:11). Emmanuel suggests that the developing nations could unite in creating their own cartels as a means of confronting the traditional hegemony of the industrial nations within the world system.

In an unusually defensive article, Arthur Lewis (1978) disagrees with the thesis of unequal exchange. Lewis argues that unequal exchange in the global economy arose not because of the persistence of colonial dependence and monopolistic practices by the West, but because of the failure of Third World countries to invest adequately in their internal production (Lewis, 1978). Perhaps. In his desperate attempt to defend the market theory of agricultural development in the developing world, Lewis ignores the fact that potential investible resources in most developing world are largely under the control of international capital. Lewis also ignores the fact that the pattern of investment in many developing societies by transnational corporations is largely determined or dictated by profit motives and not by any social or moral concern, which is outside of the realm of capitalist economic calculation.

Whatever the strengths of their arguments, the inability of dependency and world system theorists to transcend the positivism of the modernization school renders their models inappropriate or limited when it comes to understanding the persistence of economic backwardness in the Third World. Consequently, what was proposed as a science ultimately ended up as a new metaphysics in development study.

The Modes of Production Model

The failure of the world system and dependency theories to provide an adequate analysis of the class structure of Third World formations led to a new theoretical perspective, which became known as the "modes of production" school. This school recognizes 1.) that the dependency theory represents a valid, if not coherent, critique of the neo-classical modernization school of thought; and 2.) that the dependency theory remains essentially within the modernization problematic.

John Taylor (1976), in particular, contends that the inability of the center-periphery paradigm to transform the positivism and teleology found within the modernization perspective renders this paradigm an inadequate tool of analysis in the understanding of contemporary Third World economic crises. The modes of production school of thought addresses the question of the various forms of articulation within the global capitalist mode of production. By articulation, they mean a structured relation between the capitalist modes of production and the non-capitalist sectors. The modes of production approach tries to understand how these articulations shape the pattern of capitalist development on the global scale (Taylor, 1976; Amin, 1978).

According to the modes of production scholars, we must first understand how the "reproductive needs" of capital are met by the maintenance of non-capitalist sectors within the global system of production (Taylor, 1976). In other words, by retaining the pre-capitalist modes in their original forms (ensuring its ideological purity), the modes of production school argues that the dominant capitalist mode of production is able to exploit these modes to meet the conditions of its own reproduction. This idea of "reproductive needs" of capital later led to the development of the dualism thesis in which the economies of developing societies are characterized by two sectors 1.) the enclave of advanced capitalist sector, and 2.) the backward rural sector that continues to generate resources for metropolitan capitalist development. However, this dualist thesis was soon to be challenged by other radical scholars.

Introducing a new dimension to the development discourse, the Argentinian sociologist, Ernesto Laclau (1976), points to the confusion that often arises in the understanding of the processes of economic development in the Third World. For instance, the readiness of economists and sociologists alike to confuse different and separate levels of analysis may explain the inadequacy of their various paradigms. By confusing economic systems with modes of productions, Laclau further contends, sociologists often gloss over an important component that may render their analyses inappropriate

(Laclau:1976). For Laclau, an economic system comprises different modes of production and their interconnections. The modes of production, he argues, defines a specific articulation between the relations of production (mode of surplus appropriation), and forces of production (mode of expropriation of nature) (Laclau, 1971;p.37-8).

By focusing on the economic system as the unit of analysis, Laclau argues, the dependency and the world system theorists have confused contradictions that are essentially at the level of the mode of production with contradictions generated by the system of capitalist production. As a result, Laclau continues, the dualism between the advanced capitalist West and the Third World by them is seen as the defining characteristic of Third World underdevelopment. Instead, Laclau sees these contradictions as the manifestation of the effects of articulation of the global capitalist mode of production with different non-capitalist modes, and the specific pattern of accumulation defined by the relations of appropriation amongst the different modes of production within the global economy.

By conceiving economic systems as combinations of different modes of production, the argument goes, we are able to specify how their articulations result in the development of one sector of the global economy, and the "underdevelopment" of others (Taylor, 1976, Laclau, 1976). Besides semantics, Laclau's ideas are hardly different from the dualist theorists, except for describing dualism as a specific, if not inherent, characteristic of the global capitalist economic system.

In Laclau's work, and to some extent, the works of the dependency theorists, we see the quest for development in the periphery of the global economy as an impossible task because the peculiarities of capitalist development require specific modes of expropriation that can only be provided by colonial properties and external markets, which are not, according to Stavenhagen (1973), available to the developing nations. This then raises the question as to whether development is a realizable goal for many developing nations given this constrains within the world system.

Science or Ideology?

Most of these sociological theories of development have been paraded as science. The problem however is that by ignoring the historical process and the specificity of cultural conditions in the developing world, the modernization and the radical theorists, to some extent, have proposed the capitalist path to development as the most viable strategy for economic transformation. Furthermore, the assumptions of the free market economy are hardly testable; therefore, what is proposed as a science of development is nothing more than a new ideology of postcolonial subjugation and dependency. The development of Western industrialism had benefited greatly, and continues to do so, from exploiting pre-capitalist formations, mainly in the developing world.

In fact, during the different phases of western capitalist development, premodern modes of production played a very significant role in ensuring the establishment of hegemonic centers within the western metropolis. First, trans-Atlantic slavery from the fifteenth century onward provided the basis for the initial primitive accumulation for global capitalist development and the current economic might of Western industrial powers. Likewise, the transformation of slavery to a direct system of political and economic domination (colonialism) ensured the continuation of the geographical imbalance within the world system (Rodney, 1972; Onimade, 1988; p.14-18). Similarly, labor migration in the late twentieth century from the periphery to the center, and the proliferation of neo-colonial developmental ideology, all assisted, and continue to assist, in hampering indigenous capitalist development in the periphery of the world economy, most especially in black Africa.

In his seminal paper, Bade Onimade, a Nigerian political economist, describes this process most succinctly thus:

> ......while slavery accelerated any inherent crisis of dis-
> integration of African communities and destroyed tra-
> ditional technologies by the forced export of their prac-
> titioners, it vastly retarded primitive accumulation by

destroying existing forms of capital and inhibiting additional accumulation over centuries of human
exploitation...By contrast, slave looting provided an
important part of the primitive capital accumulation
of North America and Europe for launching their agricultural and industrial revolutions from the mid-18th
century. It supplied those continents with the material
precondition of accumulation and concentration of
money capital for the transition from feudal and petty
commodity producing social formations to industrial
capitalism. (Onimade, 1988; P.16).

At each turn of this process of exploitation of African social
formations, cultural imperialism replaced the use of direct
force. The proliferation of racist ideology within the world
system spelled the end of the road for a viable development
alternative for people of color worldwide. The inability of
leading theorists in western social science to acknowledge this,
and the blind commitment to a laissez- faire doctrine of stages
of progressive development, as propounded in the cumulative
equilibrium model, only revealed the entrenchment of racism
within the discipline.

Indeed, covert racism continues to structure relations
between the developed and the developing world. This system of structural inequalities between the advanced and the
developing world is often mediated through international finance institutions like the World Bank and International
Monetary Fund. These two institutions have dominated development resources and thinking since the World War II. As
expected, these instruments of the world capitalist empire have
clearly ensured the maintenance of the unequal division of labor and resources within the world system. The end result is
the perpetuation of structural dependency through the legitimation of a particular form of development ideology. This is
expressed in the current preferential lending, Structural Adjustment Program (SAP), and increasing movement of international capital to areas that were previously socialist. This
trend, however, continues to generate structural inequities
within the global system. The obvious end result of this pro-

cess is increasing world poverty, disease, and warfare in the lowest stratum of the periphery.

Furthermore, there is a partial correlation between political turmoil in the periphery and the particular form of the economic development model that is being imposed on these formations by Western imperial powers. The ugliness of war in Somalia, Rwanda, predemocratic South Africa, Haiti, and elsewhere in the periphery, is a testimony to the burden of dependency and the challenge posed by late capitalist development. This tragedy could be avoided altogether. Yet, Western social science continues to glamorize the beauty of capitalist imperialism by analyzing structures of underdevelopment in the periphery as a result of cultural attributes. This, of course, has led to the characterization of Western social science, by Third World scholars, as a form of intellectual imperialism (Ake,1980). By providing the ideological justification for the severe economic and political imbalances within the world system, social and economic sciences continue to loose their credibility as independent scholarly disciplines.

Imperialism, International Capital and Africa's Development

Lenin (1966) defines imperialism as the highest stage of capitalism, encompassing the global domination of peripheral states by hegemonic capitalist nations. This domination, originally, involved the acquisition of colonial property by the imperialist states for economic exploitation. But with the transformation of capitalism from manufacturing to finance capitalism, exploitation of peripheral states is accomplished through the dominance of finance and bank capital which, in sum, constitutes international capital. In the particular experience of African states, and perhaps with the dubious exception of South Africa, international capital's involvement with African development has produced disastrous consequences. This point has often been ignored by liberal development theorists as reflected in the works of Hokowitcz, Horton, and others. Similarly, the radical scholars failed to focus more clearly on the negative consequences of international's capital involvement in Third World development. They were merely interested in its revolutionary potential, which may be attributed to their blind ideological commitment and the lack of rigor in its theoretical schema.

Indeed, one often sees some Marxist scholars, for example Bill Warren (1980), arguing for the continuing participation of international capital in third world development, believing that such participation would result in the formation of social classes, a precondition for the socialist revolution. It is against this background of colonial plunder and continuing imperialistic exploitation of Third World resources by the hegemonic states, within the world system, that the particular character of the Nigerian crisis is examined.

Nigerian Dependent Economy

By the time of Nigerian independence in 1960, the country's economy, as left behind by the British imperial state was primarily agrarian. Despite the huge economic benefits that colonial exploitation brought to the British, very little effort was made in investing in the economy. Most investment were restricted to areas that directly benefited the British colonial state, especially sectors providing raw material and other industrial by-products to the British economy. The most profitable investments were in export related agriculture, such as the experimental cocoa plantations in the old western region, the palm oil production in the south east, rubber plantations in the mid-western region, cotton and peanut farming in the northern region .

Coal mining in the eastern region; and bauxite, tin, and other mineral resources, especially in the middle belt around Jos area, also attracted significant investments. However, long term investment were determined by political and economic factors most especially by the uncertainty of decolonization. In many parts of the country, particularly, those regions falling within the savannah and equatorial vegetation area where tropical mosquitoes were in abundance, decisions to encourage large plantations and settler farming community, like in south and eastern Africa, were unsuccessful because of the inability of European settlers to adapt to harsh tropical conditions. In the end, British colonial state encouraged local producers to specialize in export crops requiring intensive labor. This pattern of investment, as the table below shows, prevented the development of technology that could have taken advantage of local conditions and set the nation in the direction of sustained development.

Table 3.1: Cumulative foreign investment in Nigeria by type of activities (%)

Year	Mining Quary	Manufac Processing	Agric fishing	Trans Comm	Bld Const	Trade & Serv	Misc
1962	36.7	17.7	2.0	1.1	3.8	38.4	0.7
1965	43.7	18.5	1.5	1.5	5.3	24.6	4.9
1970	51.4	22.4	1.5	1.4	1.4	20.6	1.7
1972	54.7	22.7	0.6	0.8	2.2	15.1	3.6
1974	45.3	28.7	1.1	1.2	3.5	17.7	2.5
1976	39.4	23.6	1.0	0.5	5.3	26.8	3.6

Source: Onimade (1988), p.80

The majority of investments from 1962 through 1976 were in mining, trading, and business services, while fewer investments were made in infrastructures such as transportation and communications. Colonial investments in infrastructure were often limited to those areas that complemented export crop production, and they were often financed by private growers and buyers associations in Britain. The railroad networks were built to go through cocoa, rubber, and cotton plantations and bypassed rural settlements where they could have directly benefited the people. The costs of investments and interest on money borrowed to finance these railroads were directly passed down to the peasant villagers through direct and commodity taxation, even though those benefiting from the railroads were the metropolitan bourgeoisie.

In the coastal areas, especially the Lagos lagoon and the delta enclaves of the southeast, British traders followed old slave trade structures to promote commerce in timber, spice, and agricultural produce. The sort of commercial capitalism that arose out of this pattern of trading in the coastal regions served the function of incorporating the economy into the global capitalist system of production. In urban cities like Lagos, Enugu, Kano, Ibadan and Kaduna, significant manufacturing industries were established, but they were dominated mainly by British, French and Arab conglomerates such as the Levers Brothers, Patterson and Zochonis (PZ), CFAO, United Trading Company (UTC), and the United African Trading Company (UAC).

Many of these manufacturing enterprises specialized in consumer products that could be produced cheaply using local inputs. In fact, the manufacturing sectors were dominated by Lebanese and other foreigners, some of whom have settled along the West coast of Africa after the collapse of trade in human cargo. Investment in manufacturing failed to transform the economy into a modern one, instead, what one saw was the persistence of the agrarian sector of the economy, which the new nationalist elite relied on for exploitation.

At best, the class of elite that took over the control of the state after independence was caught between maintaining some aspects of the old mode of production and a rapid modernization program that would pull the economy out of total collapse. What the nationalist elite decided to do was embark on rapid urbanization at the expense of the rural sector of the economy, a decision that latter backfired, as shall be demonstrated below. What was at least clear was that one hundred years of British colonialism did not provide the basis for a program of economic revolution.

In spite of claims that colonialism transformed the economy in the direction of progress, available evidence suggests the contrary. Colonialism is a relation of political and economic exploitation, and where colonial exploiters can exploit a given social formation without disturbing its social constitutions, it will do just exactly that. In the case of West Africa, transforming the national economy in ways that might bring about progress was utterly in contradiction with the philosophy of British colonialism. While the colonial masters exploited the agrarian sector of the economy for rapid accumulation, their successors neglected rural production in favor of rapid urbanization fed by crude oil money of the seventies and eighties.

Agrarian Decline

Prior to independence in 1960, Nigeria was self sufficient in food production. This was due partly to government's concern toward the rural producers as the sole source of its revenue. For instance, during fiscal year 1954-64, the food import bill amounted to less than 10 percent of the total import bills. However, by the late seventies when agriculture was no longer the only source of revenue for the state, this figure had jumped to 18 percent (*Central Bank of Nigeria Reports, 1950 to 1965*).

By the end of the sixties, agricultural exports had declined to little less than 6 percent of total export from a peak of 86 percent in the years leading to independence (Turner and Badru, 1985). The boom in crude petroleum boom of the early seventies, contributed to the relative neglect of the agricultural sector of the economy. This agrarian decline can be seen in terms of decreasing land area under agricultural production, the increasing import of grains such as wheat and rice, the declining contribution of agriculture toward the GNP, and other related indicators as the following tables show. In the following tables, the sharp agrarian decline in Nigeria since political independence in 1960 is documented.

The decline was fuelled by sudden jump in the posted prices of crude during the Arab-Israeli war in the early seventies. During the war, oil production in the middle east fell, and the immediate response to this shortage was price hikes before production could be stabilized.

Table 3.2
Total Land Area Under Cultivation for Thirteen Major Crops ('000 ha.)

Year	Total Land Under Cultivation
1965/66	20,377
1966/67	16,196
1967/68	18,345
1968/69	18,694
1969/70	22,944
1970/71	20,336
1971/72	15,489
1972/73	19,929
1973/74	16,816
1974/75	14,939
1976/77	15,009
1977/78	11,057
1978/79	9,507
1979/80	8,626
1980/81	9,648

Source: *Federal Ministry of Agriculture, Department of Agricutural Planning*, Lagos, Nigeria, 1982.

Table 3.3

Share of Agriculture in Gross Domestic Product

Year	Total All Sectors (N.million)	Agriculture Sector (N.million)	% of Total
1956	1,747.4	1,103.6	63.16
1957	1,820.0	1,130.4	62.11
1958	1,800.0	1,239.8	68.88
1959	1,877.0	1,226.0	65.32
1960	1,962.6	1,280.0	65.22
1961	2,247.4	1,414.6	62.94
1962	2,359.6	1,453.2	61.59
1963	2,597.6	1,605.8	61.82
1964	2,745.8	1,673.8	60.96
1965	2,894.4	1,676.4	57.92
1966	3,110.0	1,691.8	54.39
1967	3,374.8	1,855.0	54.97
1968	2,752.6	1,527.8	55.50
1969	2,656.2	1,415.2	53.28
1970	3,549.3	1,711.2	48.23
1971	5,281.1	2,576.4	48.49
1972	6,650.9	3,033.7	45.61
1973	7,187.5	3,092.7	43.03
1974	12,118.0	3,352.1	27.66
1975	16,462.8	3,943.0	23.95
1976	19,437.7	4,579.5	23.56
1977	23,826.0	4,898.3	20.56
1978	26,758.5	5,143.4	19.22
1979	27,370.2	5,389.1	19.69
1980	31,424.7	5,656.8	18.00

Source: Federal Ministry of Agriculture, Information *Bulletin on Agriculture*, 1984, p.12. reproduced from Iyegha, D.A, 1988, p.32

The tables above show tremendous decline in agricultural production since the early sixties, the most significant decline coincided with peaks of oil booms especially from 1973 through to 1980. As the table below show, the same period also witnessed dramatic increases in food and grain importation to make up for shortages in internal production.

Table 3.4

Actual Food Import (1961-84) in Nigeria (N. million)

Year	Food	Vegetable oil and fat
1965	46.08	0.35
1966	51.57	0.37
1967	42.56	0.60
1968	28.39	0.58
1969	41.73	0.38
1970	57.69	0.85
1971	87.91	0.72
1972	95.10	1.06
1973	126.26	1.39
1974	154.76	3.57
1975	297.86	8.92
1976	440.93	24.69
1977	736.46	47.01
1978	1,027.11	81.26
1979	952.40	97.99
1980	1,049.05	115.00
1981	1,820.22	128.74
198	1,642.26	151.37
1983	1,296.71	105.56
1984	843.25	101.76

Source: Federal Office of Statistics, *Annual Abstract of Statistics*, Lagos

Table 3.5

Rice Production and Importation in Nigeria (1970-1979)

Yr.	Local (tons)	Importation (tons)	Total (tons)	Import Bill (N.Million)
1970	345,000	1,700	346,700	1.14
1971	383,000	300	383,000	0.05
1972	447,000	5,900	452,000	0.99
1973	487,000	1,100	488,000	0.27
1974	525,000	4,000	529,000	1.50
1975	515,000	6,700	521,000	2.38
1976	534,000	45,000	579,000	20.14
1977	667,000	413,000	1,080,000	154.94
1978	695,000	770,000	1,465,000	194.76
1979	850,000	700,000	1,530,000	121.71

Source: Reproduced from Aribisala:1983, p.8

Table 3.6

Production of Principal Agricultural Export Commodities (000 tons), 1965-1981

Year	Cocoa	Palm oil	Ground- nut.	Cotton	Beni- seed
1965/66	165	130	1385	347	32
1966/67	263	32	185	112	23
1967/68	234	4	1091	209	16
1968/69	185	na	1269	446	-
1969/70	224	na	1292	372	16
1970/71	308	na	1581	357	22
1971/72	254	na	1380	425	21
1972/73	241	na	1350	105	4
1973/74	-	na	877	85	4
1974/75	214	na	1935	481	15

Table 3.6 (con't)

Year	Cocoa oil	Palm nut.	Ground-	Cotton	Beni-seed
1975/76	-	na	458	311	15
1976/77	165	-	460	294	14
1977/78	-	na	603	269	9
1978/79	137	na	701	212	15
1979/80	-	na	453	125	7
1980/81	155	na	675	77	2

Source: Iyegha, D.A. 1988, p.38

Two reasons accounted for this trend. First, the shift in state policy from agrarian based development to one that emphasized rapid industrialization was accompanied by a shift in attitude and taste. Secondly, the discovery of crude petroleum in commercial quantity in the sixties, and the sudden jump in crude prices during early 1970s, compounded development efforts as policy makers envisaged an economic development program that would be funded by revenue from crude oil. The decision to pursue urban based development strategy could be detected in the discriminatory pattern of investment between the urban and the rural sectors of the economy.

Table 3.7: Public Sector investment , 1965-1985 (percent)

	1962-68		1970-74		1975-80		1981-85	
	p	a	p	a	p	a	p	a
Agric	3.6	7.7	9.4	9.8	6.7	7.2	12.5	-
Non-. agric.	86.4	92.3	90.6	90.2	93.3	92.8	87.5	-

Source: Federal Republic of Nigeria, *National Development Plans of Nigeria, 1962-85*. Reproduced from Iyegha, D.A. 1988, p.149.
p = Plan capital allocation; a= Actual capital allocation.

The assumption was that, once industrialization was achieved, the rural sector would in no time be transformed. As Chinzea observed:

> Agricultural policy in neo-colonial epoch in Nigeria is not markedly different from the colonial approach. The gist of the whole approach to agriculture is the accelerated investment and capitalization of agricultural production. The aim is to progressively reduce the agricultural population so as to create labor for industry. (Chinzea, 1985:55)

As Turner (1980), Onimade (1982), and Ake (1985) argued, this strategy could not produce the desired result, partly because of the peculiar incorporation of the Nigerian economy into the world system, more importantly, because of its dependent character. Indeed, widespread corruption accompanied the accelerated industrialization policy of the state (Turner, 1978). Nevertheless, crude- oil sponsored industrialization was pursued into the late seventies, despite the difficulties associated with this model. On the insistence of the neo-classical Nigerian economists, who controlled the state bureaucracy, the military administrators, in spite of popular resentments, and in the face of demonstrated failure of this strategy, continued to pursue this policy of accelerated development of the urban sector of the national economy. This marked the beginning of a new era in the direction of national economic development.

The collapse of the Nigerian national economy by the early eighties, led the state to embark on a policy of rapid agricultural revitalization. In a sense, the policy change reflects the indirect acceptance by the Nigerian state of the failure of its industrialization program. The need to concentrate on food production became the new cornerstone of the military administrators (Badru,1984; Ihimodu, 1991). In 1975, a national food program was sponsored by the administration of the military dictator General Obasanjo. It was dubbed Operation Feed the Nation (OFN). The program aimed at im-

proving peasant production through the use of fertilizers and
the introduction of high-yielding hybrid crops. Several billions
of Naira were committed to the program. As shall be shown
in the later part of this chapter, funding for the new program
did not actually go to the peasants, but into pockets and bank
accounts of senior military officers (Turner and Badru,1985).

In desperation, the military administrators summoned the
National Economic Council in 1978 charged with the responsibility of finding a solution to the agrarian crisis. The economists and policy makers in the council concluded that the rural crisis was primarily caused by the poor organization of
peasant agriculture, especially the backwardness of its production techniques, and the small size of peasant farms
(Adedeji, 1989). It recommended the displacement of peasant farming by capitalist agriculture, and the development
within the ranks of the peasants of capitalist farmers and en-
trepreneurs who would seize the advantage offered by the new
investment in agriculture.

These new policy recommendations led to the launching
of a new program, the Green Revolution. Its major beneficia-
ries, as pointed out below, were members of the military, who
sought new career in farming (Turner and Badru,1985). Indeed, the Green Revolution formed the basis for a new pattern of accumulation by the ruling elite. But this accumulation
did not lead to a transformation of the rural economy. The
Green Revolution, as argued below, only accelerated the process of rural decline partly because of poor execution and
corruption by bureaucratic officials, and wide spread corruption among the ranks of high level military officers (Badru
and Turner,1985).

State Intervention in the Economy

The concern of the Nigerian elite immediately after independence, was like their colonial predecessors, how to move peasant smallholder agriculture in a direction that would boost its
productivity. This concern, until very recently, arose out of
the need to extract more surplus from rural producers to finance state operation. In order to finance the growing bu-

reaucracy, since the government is the sole employer of labor, national plans became an effective instrument to exploit peasants' surplus produce.

During colonial times, the first bold effort to control and organize peasant production was contained in the Public Land Acquisition Ordinance of 1917, which gave the colonial government exclusive right to acquire native land for public purposes. This was followed by an even bolder Nigerian Town and Country Planning Ordinance in 1946, which empowered the colonial governor to acquire peasants' land in southern Nigeria without compensation (Olatunbosun, 1968, P.2). In northern Nigeria, similar ordinances were passed empowering colonial administrators to seize communally owned land and pass the right of ownership and use to the auspices of the colonial governors. One such ordinance was the "The Land and Natives Rights Ordinance" which empowered the colonial governor and other colonial provincial officials to administer land for commercial and public use purposes. The same ordinance also imposed tenancy fees on land occupied, and cultivated by peasant farmers thereby abrogating their rights to land (Iyegha, 1988, p.98). The overall goal of theses ordinances, as Iyegah points out, was to encourage the penetration of capitalist agriculture in the rural sector (Iyegah, 1988, p.98-106).

This pattern of encroachment of peasant smallholders' land continued after political independence. The postcolonial nationalist government pursued exactly the same strategy of displacing smallholder farmers in favor of capitalist agriculture. As Igheya notes:

> The postcolonial leaders who took over didn't change any of the rules, but promoted them to their own advantage, and to the ultimate detriment of the population... In pursuit of their priority of export crop production, the regional governments of the First Republic, through their development corporations, established cocoa, palm oil, rubber, and coconut plantations, especially, in the then three southern regions. In addition, farm settlements were founded, the aim of which

> was not only to increase cash crop production, but
> also to transform peasant farming into capitalist farm-
> ing. (Iyegah, 1988, p.99)

In the old western region alone, no fewer than forty-five plan-
tation and agricultural settlement schemes were set up, covering 34,000 acres of peasants' land. Similarly, in the former
eastern Nigeria, large plantations whose average size was between 400 and 600 acres each, were established for the purpose of growing rubber and oil palm for export (Ake,1985,
p.62). Ironically, these attempts to replace smallholder farming by large scale capitalist farms did not work as anticipated
by state bureaucrats. Except for rubber and palm oil in south
east Nigeria, it has been shown that almost all the export crops,
especially, cocoa, groundnut and beni-seeds, could be produced more efficiently in the small plots owned and run by
smallholder farmers (Clark, 1979).

The boldest attempt yet, by the Nigerian state, to displace smallholder farmers came when it introduced the Land
Use Decree No.6 of 1978. The decree, like the colonial ordinances of 1917 and 1946, vested land use, control, and administration in the hands of state military governors. The only
positive aspect of the decree was that, it undermined the traditional authority of clan chiefs, who often used land allocation authority vested in them, to enforce conformity amongst
their subjects. However, the decree, by its design, aimed at
introducing mechanized large-scale agriculture in rural areas.

For instance, in addition to the decree, the government
also simultaneously relaxed regulation that banned foreign
investors in the agricultural sector of the economy, while at
the same time playing lip service to improving smallholder
productivity (Ake, 1985, p. 64). It is within this historic battle
between the Nigerian state and peasant farmers that the analysis
of these various agricultural programs is situated.

Since 1960, no fewer than five different agricultural ex-
periments have been introduced with very little or no success. All the programs were implicitly influenced by the diffusion model. The diffusion model aimed at spreading modern
technology and Western extension advice to smallholder farm-

ers. As their names showed, all these programs reflected the desperation of the Nigerian state in feeding its population.

National Food Acceleration Production Program (NAFPP)

In the early months of political independence in 1960, the nationalist successor to British colonial administrators, agreed to using periodic national economic plans as means of ensuring sustained development. The first National Development Plan, covering the period 1962-1968, was unveiled in January of 1962. The main focus of the plan was the agricultural sector. The plan provided for an investment of 2.3 billion U.S.dollars (see *Federal Ministry of Information Bulletin*, 1962). The plan called for the establishment of farm settlement schemes, which would produce exclusively export crops. The plan barely ran its course before war broke out in 1967, resulting in its abandonment. The war broke out over unsatisfactory political arrangements that had been put into place by the British during decolonization talks with the nationalist elites.

The war lasted for four gruelling years during which agricultural production almost came to a standstill. When the war ended in 1970, a second National Plan was presented. The main features of the plan were the reconstruction of war ravaged areas and the rehabilitation of agricultural production, most especially in areas that had been ravaged by the war. A new campaign was embarked upon dubbed the National Food Acceleration Production Program (NFAPP). The campaign was launched in 1974 by the military dictator, General Yakubu Gowon. The program was put under the supervision of the Ministry of Finance with technical support coming from the International Institute for Tropical Agriculture (ITTA) in Ibadan, western Nigeria. The objective of NAFPP was far less ambitious than the farm settlement programs that were previously initiated. The emphasis was on improving peasants' productivity in staple food crops such as cassava, millet, yellow and white corn, yams, sorghum, and coconuts.

Tangentially, the campaign also emphasized the introduction of modern farming equipments, and the diversification of crops planted by smallholder farmers on a single plot. The government distributed fertilizers and other farm inputs to farmers through the extension officers of the Ministry of Agriculture. But because of poor training and inadequate supervision from qualified personnel, most of the fertilizers distributed were either improperly applied or simply left in the open sun to rot (Ogba, 1980, p.75-82). Despite the enormous investment in the NFAPP, agricultural production continued to stagnate (Table 2.3 and 2.5). The military head of state who introduced the NFAPP, General Gowon, was overthrown in 1975, and the new rulers declared the program as inappropriate and a wasteful exercise. The new military administration came with a whole new set of development ideas which were expressed in the third National Development Plan, 1975-1980.

Operation Feed the Nation (OFN)

A new plan was introduced in May of 1976 with even more fanfare than the previous ones. In the plan, 2.2 billion Naira (2.3 billion U.S. dollars, at the 1976 exchange rate) was allocated specifically for rural development. The new agricultural program favored by this new military officers was tagged Operation Feed the Nation (OFN). Emphasis was placed on mobilizing smallholder farmers for increased productivity. This was basically the same rhetoric contained in the two previous programs. The difference was the media propaganda that accompanied the launching. The new military head of state, General Olusegun Obasanjo, was shown on national television, dressed in a peasant's outfit, launching the program in a desperate effort to appeal to all segments of society. This time, the plan called for full participation of all strata of the Nigerian society in the program, and the focus was no longer on peasant farmers.

In principle, OFN was designed to redress the inadequacies and shortcomings of the previous programs without a definite concern for the smallholder farmers. The main objectives of the program were as follows:

a). To mobilize the nation toward self-sufficiency in food;

b). To encourage the section of the population that relies on buying food to grow some of its own food;

c). To encourage general pride in agriculture through the realization that a nation that cannot feed itself cannot be proud;

d). To encourage balanced nutrition and thereby produce a healthy nation;

e). To discourage rural to urban migration by encouraging young people to remain on the land;

f). To produce agricultural surpluses for sale abroad to build foreign exchange reserves. (Ogba, 1980, p.87-88)

The program was divided into two phases. The first phase was launched on May 26, 1976. This phase dubbed the propaganda phase, involved hiring 27,000 university students to "educate" peasant farmers as to the use of fertilizers, and new farm equipment like tractors and combine harvesters, which were made available to peasants' cooperatives nationwide. The second phase was launched on June 2, 1977. By this time, interest in the whole program was beginning to wane. It became obvious that a dose of revived state propaganda was necessary to move the campaign forward. Several problems plagued the implementation and administration of the program. Due to widespread corruption, inputs earmarked for the smallholder farmers were hijacked by middlemen who sold them, at below the market prices, back to unscrupulous state bureaucrats for a percentage of the cut (Turner and Badru,1985; Ogba,1980; Iyegha, 1988). Besides, agricultural loans that were to be granted to farmers could not be disbursed because of lack of collateral. In addition, the lack of adequate communication between the state OFN directorate offices and the head office in Lagos, also contributed to the failure of the program. By 1979, it became clear that this program, like its predecessors, was doomed to failure.

Meanwhile, while the military was preparing to hand over power to an elected civilian government, the operation was turned into an avenue for looting state money by military personnel who were retiring from service. Several high level military and civil officials applied for agricultural loans that were specifically earmarked for peasant farmers. Because of their personal ties and close affiliation to the programs, many of these officers simply retired and took on new careers in farming. This class constitutes what is now known as "Gentlemen farmers" in Nigeria today (Turner and Badru, 1985).

Finally, when a new civilian government was voted in toward the end of 1979, incoming politicians saw the OFN as their last chance to make it in the game of Nigerian politics. Thus, the brief civilian rule of 1979 through 1983 became a phase in Nigerian history of personal aggrandizement by corrupt politicians and officials.

Green Revolution (GR)

The last of the agricultural revitalization programs we will discuss in this chapter is the Green Revolution (GR). The program was launched, to replace the Operation Feed the Nation (OFN), in May of 1980 by the new civilian president Alhaji Shehu Shagari. The objective of this latest program, according to state officials, was " to create the means to meet the needs of the smallholder farmers and to spread the benefits of rural development" (Iyegah, 1988, p.105).

Contrary to the claims of the program's executors to focus on the smallholder farmers, the program actually ended up promoting large scale-farming. It favored absentee landlords and retired military officers in terms of loan allocation (Turner and Badru, 1985). In fact, during the entire duration of the program, many smallholder peasant farmers were displaced by new capitalist farmers and multinational corporations. These groups took advantage of the relaxation of land acquisition rules and participation by foreign investors, as contained in the Land Use Decree No.6 of 1978, to convert the new program to avenues for personal and corporate accumulation (Ake,1985; Iyegha, 1989). In fact, the disjunction between the government's proclaimed intention and the actual practice with regard to the execution of the GR was aptly put by Iyegha thus:

> Moreover, officials made public pronouncement that the smallholder would be helped in the program through subsidized fertilizer supplies, extension work, etc., on which the agricultural sector placed its hope because of the promise seen in the new civilian regime. But this federal government also continue to promote large scale agriculture; and being concerned only about the supply of food for the urban consumers. It directed its attention from the smallholder and injected huge amount of money into irrigation and the agricultural projects, some of which were already established. (Iyegha, 1988, 104)

Indeed, the Green Revolution (GR), as Onimade and other critics have pointed out, provided the basis for competition over accumulation between urban based elites and corrupt politicians of the Second Republic (Onimade,1983; Ake, 1985). The program also facilitated the penetration of foreign capital into the rural areas more than the two previous programs. The politicians in the ruling national party of Nigeria (NPN) used the GR to extend political patronage as Iyegha observed:

> The program (GR) which raised the hopes of the population turned out to be a political gimmick used by politicians to win support for their corrupt practices. It was therefore not surprising that the GR, whose institutional structure mirrored its predecessor, OFN, became an instrument by which peasants were ex-

ploited and alienated instead of mobilized. (Iyegha,
1988:105)

By 1983, the national food crisis had intensified beyond the
comprehension of even the most cynical critics of the civilian
regime (see Tables 3.3 and 3.5 above). This food shortage led
to several riots in many urban centers and, coupled with the
acrimonies surrounding the elections of 1983, the military again
intervened in the political process. In the following chapters,
we will elaborate on the civil and political crisis generated by
the deepening crisis of the Nigerian economy and the form of
state response to popular action against the military dictatorship.

Chapter 4

The Military and Politics

The Nigerian military came in to the limelight in 1965 when it seized political power from the civilian government of Sir Abubakar Tafawa Balewa, the first postcolonial president. Besides Ghana, Nigeria was one of few colonial states in Africa that did not go through a violent struggle for liberation. This seemingly smooth transition to independent nationhood overshadowed fundamental divisive issues that eventually undermined the stability of the state.

The decision of the British state to engage in dialogue as opposed to confrontation with nationalist leaders was a strategic decision to avoid a horrible war of liberation as was the case with the French in North Africa. Indeed, the defeat of French troops in Algeria, and the overwhelming rejection of the idea of "Greater France" proposed by the French imperial state in Guinea Conakry, convinced the British ruling class that a peaceful transition to independent nationhood was the surest means of maintaining economic domination over its overseas colonial dependencies.

Thus, a series of dialogues with West African nationalist leaders in the early 1950s marked the beginning of a transition to neocolonial nationhood in most of British West Africa. This peaceful transition to nationhood, in which ethnicity played a great role, laid the foundation for today's political instability. In the course of their colonization, the British ruling class saw ethnicity as a vital instrument of enforcing colonial domination. The divide and rule policy of the British colonialists in Nigeria worked well in maintaining colonial order by playing one ethnic group against the other. But with the collapse of the colonial administration, the postcolonial elites in Nigeria were soon to find out that their political constituencies were contiguous with their immediate ethnic boundaries (Nnoli, 1982). This, in effect, paved the way for ethnic animosities which were later expressed in the prolonged civil war that raged from 1967 to 1970.

The seemingly inseparable boundaries of ethnicity and political allegiance gave rise to a peculiar form of populism and political culture that were completely divorced from class. This in turn created the conditions that made military intervention in the polity inevitable. It is within this background that we try to understand the continuing presence of the military in Nigerian political culture.

The Military and Politics in the New States

The poverty of theory of the role of the military in Third World politics may be explained by the abnormality that military interventions in the political process represents for political scientists. The theoretical models that most social scientists use in explaining the role of the military in politics of the developing states are those built from the historical experience in Western democracies. The stability and continuity of western democratic forms are the subject matter of political scientists. As a result, political forms in the developing countries that do not conform to the continuity model of western democracy, are usually treated as abnormalities.

In explaining military intervention in the polity of the developing nations, Samuel Huntington (1957, 1968, 1991) sees the military as taking upon itself a modernizing role. According to Huntington, the military as the most advanced modern institution, and with an officer corps that was trained in the Western tradition, often sees its role as a modernizer. In the event of the political elite failing in their duty of moving the nation towards modernity and "catching up" with the rest of the world, Huntington argues, the military elite corps is most likely to intervene in order to save the nation from the perceived threat of disintegration.

. This modernization argument sounds convincing in the absence of any other coherent explanation. However, its simplicity and common sense approach often disguise its ideological ambiguities. This modernization model of political and economic development derives its conclusion from particular case studies, in this case, Turkey, where General Kamal Artatuk demonstrated his skill, as a modern statesman, in moving his backward agrarian society along a Western economic and political path.

However, the modernization approach could hardly explain all instances where military coups have occurred in the periphery and neither could it provide a common explanation for military interventions in societies that are so disparate in terms of their colonial experience and the specificity of their cultures. In order to overcome the assumption of the military as a universally minded modernizers other analysts have suggested a method of studying the military in its given social, economic, and geopolitical contexts.

Bill Dudley (1973) suggests that the military in the Third World emerged out of the colonial situation, and as a result, the military as a colonial institution often does not reflect the social structures of these societies. In the case of Nigeria, the military, on the one hand, reflects the ethnic configuration of the society at large with all its drawbacks, and, on the other hand, it must also perform a function of protecting its interests separate from those of other sectors of the society. These interests, according to Dudley, include protecting the pay structure of the military and ensuring promotional opportunities and other social amenities that attract individuals to join the military.

The cleavage between the middle-class in the military (officer corps), and its counter part in civil bureaucracies (political elite), Dudley contends, may derive from an attempt by the latter to undermine what the former sees as its corporate interest. The inability to resolve this cleavage, Dudley argues, may lead to the military intervening in the political process with the sole intention of protecting its corporate interest.

Michel Martin (1973), like Dudley, suggests that the military often strives to protect this corporate interest even at the expense of the other sectors of the society. And because the military barely contributes to the development of the national economy, while at the same time, it consumes a larger share of the national produce, it is inevitable that military rule alienates the section of the middle class that places emphasis on rational allocation of resources for national development. For the military to protect its corporate interests from the envy of the middle-class civilian elite, Martin argues, it must rely on extending patronage and clientelism to the this class as a means of maintaining itself in power. This in turn leads to a cycle of resentment among certain strata of the officer corps who may then mobilize the rank and file for a counter coup. However, available evidence does not often support this thesis.

For instance, in the case of the December 1983 coup, led by Major General Buhari in Nigeria, there was no evidence to suggest that the coup plotters did what they did for the love of the nation (Turner and Badru,1985). Similarly, the failed coup attempt by junior officers on April 22, 1990 had very little to do with national salvation but much to do with the personal ambitions of the young soldiers who had learned that coups are legitimate avenues for acquiring material gain. In the later case, the officers who led the coup had personal grudges against senior northern officers whom they believed were monopolizing the process of accumulation.

This is not, however, an attempt to marginalize the role personality and personal hostility plays in military coups as General Joseph Garba recalls that:

> The traditional view underplays the impact and relevance of the personalities and idiosyncrasies of the military and civilians involved. As an example, the personal relationships between General Soglo, an army chief of Dahomey (now Benin) and Prime Minister Ahomadege and those between General Idi Amin and president Milton Obote of Uganda were well known to be hostile. The plotters in each instance announce economic malaise as their motive, but the animosities between respective leaders and their army chiefs formed

the key variable. In two instances in Nigeria- during
the Shagari administration and in April 1990 during
the Babangida regime-two individuals, Bukar Zanna
and Great Ogboru, were alleged to have singlehandedly orchestrated and financed two coup attempts.
(Garba, 1995; p.143)

Nevertheless, a common mistake shared by military theorists
is their inability to provide a coherent class model of military
interventions in postcolonial Africa. Even though Dudley
(1973) talks about stratification within the Nigerian military,
he has failed to relate class affiliation of officers to the different strata of the ruling class. While the majority of Nigerian
military officers come predominantly from peasant and work-
ing- class backgrounds, the majority of them have owed their
commissions to influential members of the ruling class who
routinely intervene in the selection process. Once in power,
these officers are most likely to pursue the economic interests
of the ruling class on whose patronage the military bases its
legitimacy. This point will be elaborated further in the proceeding sections.

Colonialism and Ethnicity in Nigeria

British colonial rule in Nigeria lasted for nearly a century. Its
duration and persistence depended largely on the ability of the
British colonialists to play one ethnic group against the other.
Before 1914, what is now modern Nigeria was nothing more
than a collection of somewhat disjointed and culturally diverse people. These different cultures were initially ruled the
under three protectorates of the North, South, and Lagos.
The colonial amalgamation decree of 1914 made Nigeria a
united entity.

In precolonial northern Nigeria, there existed a rigid
class system that separated the ruling emirate oligarchy from
the commoners. The dominant ethnic groups were the Hausas
and the Fulanis who could trace their origin to northern Africa. In the South, there were the relatively egalitarian societies of the Igbos, and the semi-feudal Yoruba principalities

claiming common ancestry to a mystical legend called Oduduwa who was said to have migrated from northeast Africa and settled in Ile-Ife.

The cultural variations in colonial Nigeria was for the British both a problem and a blessing. In such an ethnically diverse geopolitical entity, creating a unified system of colonial rule was a problem. At the same time, the cultural and linguistic diversities allowed the British to impose a system of "divide and rule" that saved the British a colossal sum in colonial administrative expenses. In addition, ethnic rivalries for imperial influence created alienation and animosity among different ethnic groups to the advantage of British colonialism. As Oyobaire notes:

> Colonial rule was hardly more than a scaffolding, a superstructure over numerous pre-colonial social orders having varying degrees of independence from, and inter-dependence upon each other. The pre-colonial political cultures of authority of these social orders also varied enormously among themselves. All colonial rule did in the context of national unity was to 'amalgamate and divide' for its own purposes of domination and exploitation. (Oyobaire, 1979; p.83).

In the north, the well established class system easily provided British colonialists with judicial and administrative infrastructures that facilitated colonial rule. The emirs and other petty-officials in the emirate system were simply designated as colonial officers ruling their subjects on behalf of the British colonial state. The functions of these native officials included, among other things, collection of taxes for colonial administration, provision of native labor for colonial public works and the enforcement of colonial ordinances. Through the influence of the emirs and other lesser prefectures, local bullies were co-opted into the colonial police force (askaris). These were routinely used to enforce the new colonial order (Adamolekun, 1986).

In Yorubaland, especially in Ile-Ife, Oyo and Ibadan principalities, the semi-feudal structure also provided the British the opportunity to use the traditional chiefs whose authority over their subjects was well established before colonization. Through the chiefs and the Council of Elders (equivalent of a parliament), the colonial authority was able to set up the same system of indirect rule that worked so well in the North.

It was in the southeast of Nigeria that the system of indirect rule found its toughest challenge. Amongst the Igbos of south eastern Nigeria, there was no established system of class rule. The social structure was remarkably democratic and less hierarchical. However, this is not to suggest that there was no social or economic stratification; the point being made here is that, the decision making process, in most of the Igbo communities prior to colonization, was fairly egalitarian (cf Anikpo, 1985 and Afigbo, 1972).

In order to replicate the system of indirect rule among Igbos, it became necessary for the British to impose its own stratification system by inventing a system of warrant chiefs (Afigbo,1972). The colonial officers appointed individuals, especially traders, middlemen, and collaborators as warrant chiefs, and through them, colonial rule was enforced. The warrant chiefs were handsomely rewarded by the British who continued to provide military force to back up these new elites in situations when their authority was questioned.

William Graf (1988) contends that traditional institutions of power and authority were merely used by the British imperial power to achieve its colonial goals, and in the process, alienating the rulers from the ruled. Graf further states that:

> The traditional rulers' raison d'etre namely their organic links to their communities and their social responsibilities towards their subjects was thus further called into question, and the chiefs' role increasingly became that of enforcer and autocrat, backed by the colonial regime's law, and coercive power.(Graf, 1988;p.9)

The amalgamation decree of 1914 adequately provided the structure for indirect rule with the governor general based in Lagos coordinating all colonial administration. In essence, what the amalgamation decree achieved was the forging of a nation with little regard to existing differences, cultural, linguistic and historical. This disregard later paved the way for the tumultuous politics that followed the attainment of political independence in 1960. Indeed, the ruggedness of the political foundation upon which the new nation was built later provided the political topography which made military intervention possible. Graf observes that:

> Indirect rule actually throve upon and derived its effectiveness from the perpetuation of inter-ethnic and inter-regional differences. For the traditional rulers' authority rested largely upon their ability to maintain intact ethnic group cohesiveness, tribal customs, and distinctiveness from adjacent groups. Indirect rule tended to reinforce the most conservative aspects of traditional political organization while shutting out precolonial tendencies towards supra-ethnic group cooperation. (Graf, 1988:7)

It did not occur, perhaps, to the British colonizers that to make a viable state, all the cultural elements making up the new entity have to be drawn together in recognition of a common value system and outlook that goes beyond their separate ethnic loyalties. In fact, to unite all the different ethnic groups in a common cause of nation building would have run counter to the ideology and practice of "divide and rule" which the British colonizers found convenient at the time, and which lays today at the heart of ethnic fragmentation,...

Ethnicity and the Military

Before independence in 1960, the officer corps of the military and the police were dominated by British officers. Decolonization agreement required that the military and other para-military organizations be indigenized within two to three years of independence. In 1959, the military academy had openly stepped up its efforts to recruit and train local personnel. But because of the lopsidedness of educational development, most qualified candidates came from the two dominant southern ethnic groups, Yoruba and Igbos. It was from these groups that the first set of qualified commissioned officers were drawn.

Ethnic representation in the military created a greater challenge for the northern ruling elites. The northern elites were very smart in sensing that a political power that was not backed up by military allegiance could hardly achieve any meaningful end. Politicization of the military became the only logical way to balance to military and political power. Thus, promotions in the army and police were no longer based on seniority but on ethnic origins. As Dudley (1973) notes, the indigenization process, in the Nigeria army went a long way in exacerbating ethnic conflicts both in the military and the political arena. Dudley comments that:

> While the top command of the army (colonel and above) have been recruited from the ranks with no more than a primary education, their subordinates have been in the main, men with secondary education who have been directly commissioned . The cleavage potential of educational differentiation between the various levels of the commissioned ranks of the military becomes salient when related to promotional opportunities. (Dudley, cited in Williams, 1982)

The indigenization exercise prior to independence in 1960 favored the least qualified officers, the majority of whom were from the northern region. And with the northern domination of the parliament in Lagos, the seat of federal government, it was obvious that the end of the First Republic was in sight. The lopsidedness in promotional opportunities in the military gave rise to animosities which were generally directed against the less qualified northern officers. These animosities and ethnic sentiments expressed constantly by southern officers eventually led to one of the bloodiest civil wars in sub-Saharan Africa.

The Coup of 1966

The ethnic composition of the January coup of 1966 reflects the legacy of divide and rule that was imposed by the British colonizers. The ethnic divide imposed by the British was also replicated in all spheres of state institutions, including the military establishment. The first coup in Nigeria is very difficult to account for using the various theories of the military coups propounded by political scientists. The coup seemed to have been induced by a variety of factors, the chief of which was ethnic polarity within the military, and the increasing class differentiation within the civil society.

The leader of the January 1966 coup was an Igbo officer, Major Chukwuemeka Kaduna Uzeogwu. The other five majors were similarly drawn from the South; some of them may have been motivated by reasons beyond ethnicity. In the main, most literature suggests that the coup was planned and executed in order to forestall a political arrangement which would have favored total control of the federal structure by the northerners (cf Madiebo,1980; Ademoyega,1981).

However, reading through the account of the sole survivor of the original six majors, Major Ademoyega, one could draw the conclusion that the coup plotters were brought together by a desire to rid the nation of an inept and corrupt leadership, whose personal ambitions had led to widespread nepotism in the military. Except for Ademoyega, whose radical political ideology was formed during his student days at the university of Ibadan, the majority of the officers who took part in the January 1966 coup had personal grudges against the northern oligarchy and their collaborators in the West.

After the coup, the entire political leadership in the North had been decimated. In the military northern officers, whom the coup plotters believed received their commissions through political clientelism, were similarly eliminated. Thus, it was clear to northern officers that the coup was primarily executed to eliminate the northerners from dominating the federal political structure. This fear was reinforced by the that fact no single Igbo officer was killed during the coup. The Igbo officer, assigned to kill the army's chief of staff, an Igbo himself, refused to do so because of tribal allegiance. While the coup only lasted for more than a few days, it had indeed brought ethnicity to the fore of Nigerian politics.

In the meantime, Dr. Nwafor Orizu, acting on behalf of Dr. Nnamidi Azikiwe, the postindependence figure-head president, invited the most senior officer in the army, Major General J.T.U. Aguiyi Ironsi, to head the interim government, after the brutal assassination of the prime minister, Alhaji Tafawa Balewa. The surviving southern officers who participated in the first coup were incarcerated, while General Ironsi re-organized the command structure of the army in order to boost morale. As a gesture to the northern elite, whose leadership had borne the brunt of the coup, a young northern officer, Colonel Yakubu Gowon, was elevated and made the chief of staff of the Nigerian Army. This move, by General Ironsi, did not satisfy young northern officers who had lost faith in the concept of a united Nigeria.

In fact, in a recent account of this ugly episode, a prominent officer in the Gowon's administration, retired Major General Joseph Garba, expressed clearly the feelings of northern officers at the time when he wrote:

> At the invitation of Dr. Nwafor Orizu, General J.T.U. Aguiyi Ironsi, an Igbo, proclaimed himself the Head of State, even though he was neither the leader of the coup nor had he any inkling of its planning. This would prove to be a dilemma for him. Although he promised to consult with the people before taking any serious decisions, within a week of his coming to power he was making known his thinking on the political future of Nigeria (that this thinking is muddled and simplistic did not deter him). He then went on to issue decrees that imposed unitary government, a centralized Civil Service and abolition of the region.... His actions were characterized by a lack of consultation and were largely indecisive and placatory and made no impact either in the jubilant South or on the largely restive North. (Garba, 1995; p.145)

It was the disenchantment of the younger northern officers with General Ironsi's brief regime that led to the July
coup by these officers led my Major Danjuma. These officers
took it upon themselves to retaliate against the senseless
slaughter of northern officers in January, and in the process
captured state power. The July 1966 coup was equally as
bloody as the January one. The casualties were predominantly
southern officers, most especially, the head of state, Major
General Ironsi, and the military governor of the western region, Colonel Adekunle Fajuyi.

As the events of July 1966 unfolded, it became clear that
the intention of the northern officers was secession from the
federal union. Colonel Yakubu Gowon was installed as the
head of state at the age of thirty-two, and was immediately
mandated by the northern elite to pursue the dismantling of
the federal structure. According to undisclosed sources,
Gowon was scheduled to read a speech to the nation announcing the disintegration of the country into three autonomous
entities (Ademoyega,1981). It was later learned that the idea
of secession was opposed by the British who, through their
ambassador in Lagos, persuaded Gowon to delete the section
of his speech dealing with the secession of the North from his
radio broadcast to the nation. With Gowon installed as the
head of state, and with several senior southern officers refus-
ing to recognize Gowon's authority, the stage was set for the
bloody civil war that followed.

From August of 1966 on, events developed so fast that
most Western countries asked their nationals to restrict their
movements within the country. On the diplomatic side, the
French and the British played the most significant part in the
unfolding crisis. The two imperial states were very much concerned with what would happen to crude petroleum exploration once the country was split into various parts as it ap-
peared imminent then. In south east Nigeria, where the entire
crude petroleum deposits were located, the military governor
of eastern region, Colonel Emeka Odumegwu Ojukwu, had
clearly shown his intention to cut the rest of the country off in
his secessionist bid. The major petroleum concession holders

were French and British multinationals, and the imperial powers had conflicting views about the emerging crisis.

For the British, the idea of the East seceding from the federation was not practicable. But for the French, such an idea was not only real but also to the best interest of French capital, particularly in the petroleum industry, which had been monopolized by the British. In fact, the French through their ambassadors in Lagos and through other third party intermediaries, had promised not only to give recognition to the new independent nation of Biafra that Colonel Ojukwu was proposing, but also offered to fund the new state in case of a military showdown with the federal forces. While the British did not initially show interest in supporting any of the warring factions in the military, it was clear that it was waiting to see which way the western region would go in case of a northern declaration of war on the East.

Before the end of 1966, ethnic animosity had manifested itself in organized pogroms of Igbos in northern Nigeria. By this time, Colonel Ojukwu had convened a meeting of the Igbo elders in Enugu, where he was given the mandate to create an Igbo sovereign state that was later to be known as Biafra. In early 1967, several Igbos returning from the North painted an ugly picture of massacre, rape, mayhem, and illegal incarceration, which they had suffered in the hands of the Hausas and Fulanis. The Igbos also responded by killing any Hausas they could lay their hands on, and with very little progress in the areas of arbitration which had been organized by the political elites, and with promises of weapons and money from the French in return for unlimited crude oil exploration, the stage was set for secession. Thus, on May 30, 1967, Colonel Ojukwu, the rebel military governor of Eastern region, declared Igboland and its adjoining territories the independent republic of Biafra.

Two weeks later, the northern led army declared a swift and short "police action" to capture Colonel Ojukwu and to put an end to the secession. A full-scale war, however developed which lasted for four years, claiming nearly six million lives. The stage thus was set for the legitimation of military rule in Nigerian politics. It is the politics of this military power and its class basis that we choose to analyze in the following chapters.

Chapter 5

The Civil War

The pervasiveness of ethnic problems within the military, and the failure by the officer corps to resolve serious ethnic antagonisms within its rank and file led ultimately to the bloody civil war. While there are no reliable figures for the numbers who died during the four years of the most macabre war country ever experienced, estimates range from one to three million. The majority of those who lost their lives were ethnic Igbos of southern Nigeria, who to this date, are still being treated as second class citizens by the two major ethnic groups. The ethnic sentiments unleashed by the killings of civilian leaders, during the first and the second coups, created the conditions for the pogrom of Igbos in northern Nigeria after the coup of 1966.

The contradictory accounts of the war reflect deep ethnic allegiance on the part of those who have recorded the history of the civil war. Indeed, most of the written accounts of the war have come primarily from military officers who took part in the planning of the various coups that culminated in the prolonged rule of General Yakubu Gowon. Most of these accounts are lacking in class analysis of the events that led to the civil war. In fact, not a single account of the war by these officers was able to analyze the kind of class alliances that were forged while the war was being prosecuted.

The reason for this failure to provide an accurate account of the war may be due to the fact that these officers were writing from a military perspective and a personal desire to deal with specific issues raised by other fellow officers in their various accounts. Except for the accuracy by Major Ademoyega's, the sole survival of the original six majors who led the first coup, all existing written accounts of the war gave ethnic reasons for the coup that overthrew the government of Alhaji Abubakar Tafawa Balewa and for the subsequent civil war. This chapter, therefore, looks at the various actors, class conflicts, and working class consciousness, which this author believes are pertinent to explaining the civil war and consolidation of dictatorial power by General Yakubu Gowon.

Class or Ethnic Consciousness?

In the previous chapter, it was suggested that the preponderance of ethnic issues may provide us with a window to understanding the political crisis that embroiled the First Republic immediately after independence in 1960. However, ethnicity by itself cannot be a sufficient explanation. This is because of the fact that, behind the facade of ethnic politics of the nationalist elites there were fundamental class contradictions. In the Nigerian context, ethnicity goes beyond group identification; solidarity determines the relationship of power and resource distribution which Nnoli describes as follows:

> Ingroup-outgroup boundaries emerged with (ethnicity) and, in time, become marked, more distinct than before, and jealously guarded by the various ethnic groups. Acceptance and rejection on linguistic-cultural grounds characterize social relations. These are expressed inevitably through interethnic discrimination in jobs, housing, admission into educational institutions, marriages, business transaction or the distribution of social welfare services. The factor of exclusiveness is usually accompanied by nepotism and corruption. (Nnoli 1978, p.7)

The pervasiveness of ethnicity in the Nigerian social formation has undermined class solidarity because potential class issues are often analyzed and articulated in ethnic terms. This has allowed for the fragmentation of the struggle for justice and equitable distribution of power and resources, which may explain why opposition to military rule has failed, so far, to achieve its concrete objective.

However, despite the pervasiveness of ethnicity, the First Republic, which was headed by a northerner, Alhaji Tafawa Balewa, could hardly be described as a class neutral government as some authors have suggested (cf Nnoli, 1978). Indeed, it could be argued that prior to colonization, class formation was progressing along lines that made European conquest possible. To suggest otherwise is synonymous to reducing the history of class contradictions in the Nigerian society to colonial rule.

For instance, in northern Nigeria, with its history of participation in the trans-Sahara trade that originally linked North Africa to the world system of capitalist production, class formation had developed to a remarkable degree Usman, 1979). By class formation, we refer to the development of specific relations of exploitation giving rise to a class of exploiters and the class of exploited in a determinate social formation. The terms of exploitation are determined by a definite and structured relationship of social actors to the means of production of social life such as machinery, capital, and land. The emergence of Hausa and Fulani traders, as participants in the trans-Saharan trading network in the fifteen and sixteenth centuries, made the northern town of Kano a commercial center within the emerging capitalist world system, incorporating the development of social classes distinguished by differential access to commercial capital and land.

While majority of these traders could trace their roots to northern nobility and specific Islamic ruling circles, significant number of commoners also took part in the trans-Sahara trade. These groups of actors were later transformed into the new commercial class during early period of colonization. The merchant class, as we choose to refer to these trading elites, owed their independent existence to powerful emirs and to various caliphates in the provincial centers within which they operated. The show of allegiance to the political authority of the emirs was often demonstrated by the merchants' generous

donations to the emirate courts and their philanthropic mag-
nanimity to provincial Islamic mosques. Islamic fundamental-
ism was put at arms length by the craftiness of the emirs who
provided for the material needs of the radical Islamic scholars in addition funding patrons to Islamic mosques.

Similarly, with the collapse of the trans-Atlantic slave
trade, the majority of the merchants moved their capital further north and, in alliance with Arab capital, this class was
able to finance clandestine trade in slaves. In the period of the
trans-Atlantic slave trade, the northern merchant capitalists
were freely moving their capital from one profitable venture
to the other. In the South, freed slaves, who had migrated
southeast from Sierra Leone and Liberia to the Lagos coast-
line, were busy participating in coastal trading including clandestine slavery. In alliance with powerful Yoruba and Benin
chiefs, freed slaves were also busy accumulating capital by
participating and transforming themselves into middlemen
between inland peasant produce producers and European and
Arab merchants along the coast (Ajayi, 1985).

In the hinterland, especially the Yoruba heartland, inter
tribal wars had also led to the emergence of powerful ruling
houses and trading elites who connected the Yoruba warlords
with European slave traders. However, the process of class
formation, particularly in southern Nigeria, intensified with
the direct colonial rule and the amalgamation decree of 1914.
Traditional chiefs, who oversaw provincial colonial administration, especially in Igboland of southeast Nigeria, used their
power and position to acquire wealth and peasants' land. In
the eastern region, corrupt Igbo warrant chiefs openly abused
their power in violation of native law to acquire wealth and
property (cf Afigbo, 1972).

By the end of colonial rule in the early sixties, these privileged individuals across the country had accumulated reason-
able capital to the extent that they became a tangible social
force during the decolonization period. Finally, the colonial
bureaucracy also allowed some individuals, associated with
the colonial administration, to accumulate capital through
fraudulent means. The extension of universal education to the
masses also played a part in the creation of an educated elite

class. These were lawyers and journalists, who fought for the control of the colonial state. Finally, the extension of colonial capital into agro-processing industries in the provincial municipal centers of Lagos, and Kano is often under- estimated by some observers. For instance, British colonial capital's involvement in meat and cotton production for export in northern Nigeria, cocoa export in the West, and palm kernel and oil palm export in the south eastern Nigeria resulted in the creation of a significant class of industrial workers in urban centers.

Politics in the First Republic

If we accept the above analysis, then we can begin to understand the politics of the First Republic in its proper class perspective. Parliamentary representation in the federal house in Lagos, during the First Republic, was dominated exclusively by members of the northern oligarchy or their representatives. The Prime Minister, Sir Alhaji Tafawa Balewa, was wielding political power on behalf of the Emir of Sokoto, Sir Ahmadu Bello, who was the regional governor of the North. The National Peoples Congress (NPC) was the party that represented the economic interest of the northern oligarchy and the merchant class. However, party politics was largely, but not entirely, based on ethnicity.

As was noted above that the northern merchant class derives its political and economic power from the ruling houses in the North, it can be no surprise that the coalition formed under the umbrella of the NPC was to dominate the political arena in Nigeria immediately after independence in 1960. The constitution that was forced, by the British on postcolonial Nigeria was one that not only recognized the political primacy of the northern oligarchy but also affirmed its economic dominance.

The southern opposition in the federal parliament were represented by two political parties. The National Council of Nigerian Citizens (NCNC), led by Dr. Nnamdi Azikwe, was an uneasy coalition of parties representing the economic interests of the Igbo merchant class and the warrant chiefs. Their political demand was limited to participation in the postcolonial bureaucracy and the expansion of business opportunities for the nouveau rich Igbo and Yoruba merchants.

The other party, Action Group (AG), whose populist leader, Chief Obafemi Awolowo, only aspired for the control of federal power for the purposes of executing personal agendas, failed to galvanize the support of the Yoruba elite. While claiming to be the party of poor peasant farmers, AG was, indeed, a party of privileged elite with very strong ties to metropolitan merchant capital. Of the three political parties, the NPC was the only party that showed some degree of class unity and organizational cohesion, and, as a result, it was able to take advantage of the conditions created by the colonial state to achieve its own economic and political aspiration. Intra-class struggle within the AG, especially the failure of the merchant class to establish its hegemony over the party, consequently led to its disintegration, and the subsequent civil strife, in the former western region during the early sixties.

The political crisis that overshadowed the transition to independent nationhood in late 1950s was quickly resolved when class compromises were made between the northern oligarchy and the comprador merchants in the southeast. The compromise led to the appointment of the leader of the NCNC, Dr. Azikwe, as head of state without much political clout, while the Prime Minister, Sir Abubakar Tafawa Balewa, effectively controlled political power at the federal level.

The same class compromise also led to the marginalization of the leader of the AG, Chief Awolowo, whose only support lay in the tiny ethnic constituency that he had in the western region. Once this alliance was concluded between the southern merchant class and the northern landed oligarchy, the stage was set for the ethnic struggle that later degenerated into civil war. By then, crude revenue became a serious issue in regard to the distribution of federal funds to the regions. The southern enclaves, where most of the crude resources are located, became the locus of the war.

Whose War ? Genocide and Barbarism

As mentioned above, several books have been written about the Nigerian war that claimed the lives of three million or more innocent peasants; none of these accounts have questioned the moral basis of the war. The question that all of these books have been unable to answer is: Whose war was it? The answer is simple, It was the elites' war of greed fought over the private distribution of petro-dollars.

The war broke out, as mentioned in the previous sections, amidst confusion over the ethnic composition of the regime of General Yakubu Gowon. But as the war progressed, it became clear what class interests were at stake. The council of civil commissioners that was set up during the early phase of the war by Gowon played an important role in the prosecution of the war. In order to secure the support of the Yorubas, Chief Obafemi Awolowo was released from prison to become the federal commissioner for finance. Awolowo had been previously charged, convicted and sentenced to life imprisonment for treason by Balewa's government. Thus, General Gowon was able to portray the war as a just war to the international community, and increasingly, military propaganda continued to stress that the survival of the Nigerian nation depended on the successful prosecution of the war.

By consolidating the power of the civil commissioners, General Gowon had displaced the economic power of the merchant class, and in the process, strengthened the power of state bureaucrats and senior civil servants. The civil servants, in particular, played a significant role during the first fifteen months of the crisis. As the war progressed, the civil servants were replaced by another set of social actors who had strong connections to international capital. Indeed, some observers have argued, that the replacement of the civil servants as decision-making functionaries with civilian commissioners marked a new beginning in a desperate attempt by Gowon to seek legitimacy for his crisis ridden government. As Adamolekun observes:

> A reorganization of the federal executive council to
> include civilian politicians was widely interpreted to
> mean that the military leaders saw a need to appeal for
> support from the civilian population..... "With civil-
> ians brought into key decision making positions, the
> civil population became formally committed to, and
> identified with, the purposes of the federal government
> and the federal military." (Adamolekun 1986, p.104-
> 105)

Competition within the elite class over the sharing of war generated booty was limited to the procurement of armaments
and supplies to the military. The civilian commissioners and
civil bureaucrats fought over the accumulation process, while
foreign capital played one group of actors against the other.
During the duration of the war, the national bourgeoisie consolidated their grip on state power. Several corrupt military
commanders also accumulated capital by diverting resources
meant for the war to private accounts and by pocketing the
pay checks of dead soldiers under their command.

As the war waged on, the competition between civilian
commissioners and civil servants deepened. At every turn,
the civil servants attempted to usurp the power of the commissioners by resurrecting the process of accumulation in the
direction of the merchant class. This excessive corruption and
graft, during and immediately after the war, led to the decline
of Gowon's popularity among junior officers and civilians who
did not benefit financially from the war. Government contracts were usually given out to close associates of the dictator. By and large, Gowon's continuing hold on power depended
largely on the support of senior military officers who had accumulated enormous wealth through kickbacks on government contracts. Generalized abuse of power by Gowon's civilian ministers led to civil litigations across the country, and
the government response was the enactment of more draconian
decrees that made jail term mandatory for those bringing litigation against government officials.

The Military Control of Crude Oil and Accumulation

The war saw a temporary disruption of oil production. War efforts were financed exclusively by borrowed money with promises that such money would be repaid at the end of the war. By the time the war ended in 1970, the struggle among the civilian bureaucrats had taken on a new meaning. At best, the senior civil servants-the so-called super secretaries-paid lip service to the civilian commissioners, bypassing them to deal directly with the head of state, General Yakubu Gowon.

By 1974, the civilian commissionaires were nothing more than figure heads in the ministries while real power lay within the circles of the super secretaries. It was, according to some observers, the super secretaries who advised Gowon to re-negc on his promise to return the country to civil democracy (Adamolekun 1986). In 1975, General Gowon was overthrown after years of economic mismanagement and corruption. Gowon's overthrow led to a shifting of the accumulation process in the direction of the comparator bourgeoisie. A triangular relationship, comprised of state bureaucrats, foreign capital and the merchant class was to dominate the process of accumulation, which was made possible by the new found wealth in crude petroleum (Turner 1976).

The fall of General Gowon reflects the contradictions and intra-class struggles between the comprador elements and the rising national bourgeoisie. The economic dominance of the national bourgeoisie was affirmed during the brief rule of the slain populist soldier, General Murtala Muhammed. Under General Muhammed's brief rule, when the hegemony of the comprador and metropolitan capital was challenged. For instance, General Muhammed was able to push through the Armed Forces Ruling Council (AFRC), the implementation of the Indigenisation Decree of 1975, which nationalized British interests in BP-Shell, the crude oil conglomerate. However, the partial nationalization of the crude sector, by the populist actions of General Muhammed, should not been seen as a socialistic agenda on the part of the military as William Graf comments:

> The "nationalization" of the selected sectors of the
> economy cannot be equated with the 'socialisation' of
> the economy in general. Indigenisation is part of an
> over all programme of elite accumulation within the
> parameters of the given socio-economic order. It is not,
> and has never aspired to be, a programme of social
> and economic redistribution and transformation geared
> toward the resolution of the structural contradictions
> alluded to above. In particular, it reflects the necessity
> for state intervention to strengthen indigenous capital
> vis a vis foreign capital and to compensate for the in-
> experience of local capitalists. (Graf 1988;57).

Indeed, the Indigenisation Decree was seen by the national bourgeoisie as an opportunity for that class to partake more effectively in the process of accumulation. At the same time, the military leaders who pushed through the indegenisation decree, in spite of strong protestations from the American and the British, were able to articulate a more radical foreign policy, which attacked Washington's interference in the country's affairs. However, this open confrontation with Washington was to mark the beginning of the end for General Muhammed because of his boldness in attempting to curtail the power of international capital.

The turning point came on February 13, 1976 when General Muhammed was assassinated by disgruntled elements in the army who thought that the General was going too far with his "socialist" program. But it later became clear that the junior officers who killed General Muhammed were paid agents of foreign governments. General Olusegun Obasanjo, the joint chief of staff, who took over federal executive power after the assassination, was to radically change the shape of politics in Nigeria by redefining class relations to the neocolonial state. Under Obasanjo, two significant developments are worthy of note. First, Obasanjo undermined the traditional base of the feudal oligarchy by promulgating the 1978 Land Use decree that was mentioned above. Second, a new class of capitalist farmers emerged from the ranks of retired civil servants and military officers challenging the economic and political dominance of the comprador class (Turner and Badru, 1985). This class of "gentlemen farmers" was later to play a significant role in the rise and fall of the Second Republic.

The regime of General Obasanjo was hopelessly short on ideas and over-ambitious in terms of its vision of a new Nigeria. The regime embarked on incredibly fame seeking development projects that allowed international capital and local bureaucrats to plunder the national treasury, which had already grown dramatically with the escalating price of crude oil (Turner, 1980). In the crude petroleum sector, the situation was near anarchy as the comparator elite connived with international capital to steal from the nation several billion in oil revenues. There was little or no supervision of the crude oil sector that allowed multinational oil corporations to exploit oil without the slightest regard to federal regulations. Meanwhile, members of the comprador class were engaged in ceaseless oil bunkering, with the support of the military junta; in the process, they enriched many top military officers.

Toward the end of 1978, as the transition program of the military was nearing its end, the Nigerian National Oil Corporation (NNOC) came directly under the office of the head of state. As was later learned, many oil contracts were signed without proper records. At the time General Obasanjo left office in 1979, a hefty sum of $2.8 billion was reported missing from the accounts of the NNOC. Before leaving office in 1979, Obasanjo hurriedly conveyed a constitution drafting assembly, which was comprised of mainly members of the comprador class. The assembly produced a self- serving constitution that formed the legal basis of the Second Republic.

By the summer of 1979, indications from the crude oil market pointed to a bleak future. The crisis of 1975 and 1976 was a forerunner to this disaster. The Nigerian economic managers either closed their eyes to this impending gloom or could not grasp the magnitude of the crisis and the extent of corruption and graft in the oil sector. Despite increases in the world market price of crude oil and the enormous accumulation from crude oil, the national economy never turned around. While growth in the oil sector rose by 31.3 percent, growth in the non-oil sector grew only by 7.4 percent in 1974 and 1975.

This shows that the non-oil sector of the economy was hardly responding to the bustling activities in the oil sector. This apparent inertness of the national economy has been variously blamed on: 1). incompetent economic managers and the lack of the spirit of entrepreneurship; 2). corruptions and excessive control of the economy by the government (Schartz, 1984; Browsberger, 1983). These explanations ignored the essential attributes of the Nigerian economy, most especially its dependent character and its satellite status within the world system.

In sum, the argument of this chapter is that political formation under the military continues without resolving the ethnic problems that led to the civil war. Successive military rulers have relied on a formula of representation that attempts to incorporate members of various groups into the federal cabinet in order to prevent the revival of ethnic riots. This formula has only worked to the extent that it has driven ethnic agitations under the carpet. In the process of doing this, the military has managed to maintain its own hegemony over civil society. But how long the center will hold together is impossible to assess at this juncture in Nigerian history.

Chapter 6

Economic Crisis and State Repression

The economic crisis during the Shagari regime, 1979-1983, set the course for the current crisis of polity, economy, and society in Nigeria. Corruption amongst the political elite, and economic mismanagement by state bureaucrats, during this brief civilian administration, made business for international capital difficult and uncertain. The transition from military to civilian rule in 1979 initially received full support and, in fact, impetus, from the U.S. and other western powers. This followed from the need for legitimation of the political process in Nigeria where profits were high, especially for Western oil capital.

However, the civilian regime of Shagari, and the subsequent seven month military regime of Buhari, refused to embrace the Structural Adjustment program (SAP) of the IMF and World Bank as the economic crisis intensified. Subsequently, international capital, in collaboration with internal social forces, helped usher in the more compliant military regime of General Ibrahim Babangida in August 1984. In recognition of the support he had received from international capital, Babangida adopted the IMF's nine-point program SAP, despite a national debate that culminated in recommending otherwise.

In 1986, Babangida announced his intention to hand over power to a civilian government by 1992. According to the military leadership of this 88.5 million strong oil-rich, but heavily indebted, giant of Africa, elections would be part the transition to democracy. For example, revenue from oil fell dramatically from $25 billion in 1980 to barely $6 billion in 1984 while at the same time, external debt rose from $3.4 billion in 1978 to $30.7 billion in 1988 (Garba 1995, p.43). As is currently the practice, receiving economic assistance from the International Monetary Fund (IMF) requires a sort of political democratization. In the international political lexicon, such "democratization" goes hand in hand with the "market liberalization" which opens the domestic economy to international capital. Paradoxically, market liberalization has necessitated both curbing state economic activity and expanding state political control over the turbulence which accompanies privatization.

This study argues that the military transition program in Nigeria was a ploy by international capital, in collaboration with the Babaginda regime, to produce an apparently democratic state which, in fact, would function as a repressive agency for global capital accumulation. Indeed, under the rubric of democratization, linked with a speedy economic recovery, the Nigerian government has denied its political opposition opportunity for debate and has suspended human rights.

Theoretical Perspective

The perspective on human rights presented here is both material and structural. We understand human rights as part of the broader question of how law, its enforcement, and the state are connected with global and local imperatives for capital accumulation. Rather than any deterministic causality, there is a reciprocity of conditioning circumstances, which embraces the world market, the national state and local classes. In this connection, James Petras and Morris Morley have pointed out that:

> It is not only the world market that socializes actors, thereby limiting outcomes, but also the classes themselves. Their institutions, struggles and collective consciousness are inserted into the accumulation process

and shape the conditions under which markets operate. It is this movement upward - from the basic class unit in the national social formation mediated by the state and acting upon the world market and, in turn, acted upon by the market mediated by the state - that shapes the political choices in the modern world. (Petras and Morley 1990, p.43)

Since 1978, the international economy has been in deep crisis. During this period, higher profits have been sought, and this has stimulated expansion to the periphery which has further necessitated a reversal of the economic nationalism that expressed through OPEC and other commodity associations during the seventies. At the same time, debt in the periphery was mounting rapidly, notably in the oil producing and exporting Third World states, under regime of low interest rates. In Nigeria, there was the dominance of multilaterized international capital, most especially the oil corporations. There was also a proliferation of investment by finance capital as the demand for national and international banking grew. Several multinational corporations moved into agriculture. Lever Brothers and UAC, for example, established major plantations to produce commercial crops such as rubber, palm oil, and cotton in Nigeria. Increasingly too, oil capital has moved rapidly into agribusiness to take advantage of present economic difficulties.

This movement toward agribusiness by transnational corporations has only strengthened the structure of economic dependence which had been established in the earlier period. This strengthening of dependence reflects the inability of the national bourgeoisie to engage in productive investment. Competition with international capital was not possible and the national bourgeoisie remained weak and often moved capital from production into commerce. This is consistent with the oil boom reality under which the most profitable kind of capitalist business was commerce.

Most of the development projects which Nigeria executed during this period were engineered and planned by international capital. The emphasis was on infrastructure (roads, airports, electricity expansion, telephone, and other types of communications, port development, and an expansion of educational institutions). But this period also saw the emergence of an alliance between international capital and comprador capital, and this alliance dominated the Nigerian state (Turner and Badru, 1984). Because of its structural location within the economy, there was very little room for the national bourgeoisie to embark on promoting a viable capitalist production.

Oil Based Economy and the Rise of New Classes

By early 1970s, new ranks of comprador bourgeoisie were beginning to emerge. Some of these made their money from fronting for international capital, while others were involved in oil bunkering, colluding with state officials and the military. Many of these comprador bourgeoisie accumulated capital from commerce and from state contracts to invest in production, mainly light manufacturing (textiles, bottling, paper products, soap). Some army officers moved into capitalist agriculture, while others moved into cement production and construction. Some also moved their money into oil servicing businesses.

While the rate of urbanization accelerated, the average minimum wage rose, and the strategic section of the working class witnessed improvements in its standard of living. This was especially dramatic among the thousands of oil workers and oil industry service workers. Many men from the countryside secured wage work in the booming construction business which was probably the main feature of the period of abundant oil revenues. The attraction of the city to country dwellers resided mainly in the promise of jobs; but for many, this dream was not realized. Thousands of unemployed people concentrated in slum ghettoes and were reduced to feeding themselves from the refuse in the streets. The level of working class violence in the form of armed robbery, dubious business undertakings, drug dealing and prostitution skyrocketed. With this rapid transition, the innocence and order of the past was jettisoned for a violent, uncertain, and insecure nightmarish reality which, for most urban residents, constituted the new Nigeria.

The rural sector during this period was neglected in large part because the government depended on oil revenues, not sales revenue from export crops. The neglect, lack of investment in basic rural infrastructure, and the out-migration of rural men created the conditions for a severe rural crisis, characterized by a dramatic drop in production. Nigeria became a major food importer. Women felt the brunt of this deterioration of the rural economy most strongly.

Oil Burst and International Capital

In the international economic arena, a deep recession and debt crisis shook the foundations of the capitalist system, notably through the financial institutions. International monetary instability was further undermined by debt repudiations and the reluctance of many Third World governments to renegotiate debt payments under terms which would almost certainly stimulate political turmoil threatening their own survival. In the Eastern bloc, the unrest escalating after 1988 led to the ouster of communist party regimes and the breakup of Comecon.

The result was a tremendous expansion of the world market and an expansion of the realm of operation open to international capital. However, political instability and the absence of legal and other frameworks within which corporations could guarantee property rights, profit repatriation, and other priorities of global accumulation hindered the ability of international capital to realize the potential of this tremendous market expansion.

The international ideological response to the breakdown of state capitalism in the Eastern bloc was to champion democratization. In practice, "democratization" referred to bourgeois liberal democracy, but it was a slogan of immense attraction to people of all classes in Africa and elsewhere in the developing world who were languishing under the boot of military repression.

In order to address the question of Third World debt, the world Bank and IMF introduced debt equity swaps, debt buyback, and debt conversion. In each of these cases, the idea was for international capital to convert debt into equity in the countries which are owing. For instance, with respect to Nigeria, the mechanism of debt equity conversion could mean that international capital could now control business operations previously owned by the Nigerian state in an amount equal to all or a negotiated proportion of the value of the Nigerian debt which currently stands at $38 billion. This dramatically removed sovereignty from the indigenous classes and from the local state.

In essence, the nation went into a state of receivership, being administered and directed from abroad, and, in particular, from the planning offices of the World Bank, IMF, and those private firms to which these international organizations contract out such management functions. Combined with rigorous privatization, this process led to the elimination of state capital or at least to its contraction, and the rise of a new kind of business alliance.

In agriculture, retired military officers have long dominated major agricultural enterprise. With the introduction of the SAP, increasingly large numbers of foreign multinationals began moving into commercial crops (Lever Brothers, UAC, and some oil multinationals such as Texaco). With the active collaboration of the state, the multinationals have had little difficulty in obtaining expanded acreage from ordinary peasant farmers. As a result, a mass of landless laborers has emerged in the countryside, exacerbating the agrarian crisis. Moreover, while multinational involvement led to increased export crop production, the impact on food production for the domestic market was disastrous. As a direct consequence of SAP-related policies, malnutrition and disease have increased throughout the society with women and children bearing the brunt of it.

State Revenue Crisis

By the early 1990s, international capital had decisively asserted its hegemony over the Nigerian state. The comprador class had little option but to align itself with international capital on a new basis, one devoid of nationalism. The terms of the preexisting alignment were renegotiated by foreign partners such that the new dispensation was very much more in the interests of international capital. The execution of the SAP was the beginning of this realignment. The financial crunch was the whip which drove the now dangerously indebted neocolonial state into the hands of international finance institutions. Privatization hit parastatals such as the postal services and telecommunications. By 1990, some 55 publicly-owned enterprises had been sold to private investors (World Bank 1991, p.402). In addition, over 400,000 new shareholders had been created under the privatization program.

By 1990, public sector debt had reached US$ 35 billion, which represented 107 percent of gross domestic product (GDP). The debt service is practically one quarter of total foreign exchange earnings (World Bank 1991, p.404). The state, in short, has lost what autonomy it had. This fundamental undermining of national sovereignty is vividly reflected in the breakdown of the judicial system, the disappearance of due process, and the abrogation of fundamental human rights. There is, thus, a direct connection between the strategies of international capital, as expressed in particular through SAP, and the status of human rights in Nigeria, as in many other Third World societies.

The comprador class has addressed the economic crisis of the world economy and the oil bust by aligning itself more closely with international capital. The 1984 Babangida coup thwarted attempts by retired military to enter into agriculture. Comprador accumulation was the fall back option, and many of these would-be producers turned to commerce as a last resort. The national bourgeoisie contracted, as no spare parts could be imported to operate the factories. The foreign exchange crunch made dependent industrial development impossible, and, as a consequence, national infrastructure fell into disrepair.

Structural Adjustment for Whom?

As it has been argued above, the adoption of the SAP adjustment program laid the foundation for the political repression that was to follow. But the question is whose interests are being realized by the adoption of this program? The best way to deal with this question is to look at the key elements of the program itself.

The introduction of SAP, officially in mid-1987, was intended to stem the tide of economic decline after the sudden drop in revenue from crude oil. Sensing that the national sentiment was against the implementation of any externally imposed economic policies, the military, in late 1986, announced a series of fiscal policies which were designed to readjust the national economy without borrowing money from the World Bank. But these polices were an exact replica of those prescribed by the World Bank and the IMF, under the SAP arrangement. While the previous governments have been cautious in implementing the program, General Babangida cleverly announced a transitional agenda while at the same time committing to a speedy recovery of the economy by making a case for a viable economic base for democratization.

SAP included nine policies or what the Bank officials chose to call "conditionalities". The execution of all of these policies will qualify the country for a new round of lending from the IMF and allow the Nigerian state a breeding space to work out a new debt rescheduling arrangement. The "conditionalities" can be briefly summarized as follows:

1. devaluation of the national currency and the abolition of foreign exchange control;
2. fiscal anti-inflationary policies that call for removal of subsidies on essential items including petroleum;
3. reduction of state spending on social services such as health and education;
4. trade liberalization, maintaining an open door to in-

vestment and importation of foreign goods;

5. privatization of public enterprises (parastatals) and sale of government   shares in private companies;

6. open door policy for multinational corporations including free repatriation of accumulated profits;

7. monetary anti-inflationary polices, including, but not limited to, control of bank lending and higher interest rates;

8. control and reduction of wages paid to labor;

9. anti-inflationary dismantling of price controls and minimum wages.

When fully implemented, the program is expected to generate positive results in the economy in addition to accomplishing the following objectives:

1). to raise the rate of utilization of existing installed capacity in agriculture and industry;

2). to accelerate food production and rural development and encourage the use of local raw and intermediate materials;

3). to gear fiscal and economic policy to growth through tax incentives and growth-oriented commercial policy and, by re-organizing the tariff, to make it less restrictive and more competitive.

4). to reform the public service, making it more efficient, and through privatization and commercialization of government enterprises where appropriate, reducing the scope of government of government intervention;

5). to promote job security by widening employment opportunities;

6). to keep the external debt service to a limit of 30 percent of export earnings. (Okigbo 1989, p. 176)

The overall effect of these bizarre policy recommendations by the IMF, supported by the World Bank, was in the opposite direction of its anticipated goals. It has in fact reduced capacity building and certainly produced disastrous consequences for Nigeria's dependent economy as inflation continues to quadruple, workers' retrenchment becomes part of daily life. There is a catastrophic fall in the standard of living of most Nigerians, while state policy continues to enhance the economic advantage of the elite class, the military brass and international capital (Adepoju, 1993).

Indeed, these fiscal policies, wherever they have been executed in the Third World, have rarely been successful in restructuring national economies (Hutchful,, 1989). It has been shown that these polices have complicated the efforts towards sustained development in the developing societies of the South while at the same time consolidating the economic advantage of international capital (Onimade, 1988; Hutchful, 1990). Since the adoption of the SAP, prices of basic consumer commodities have, in some cases, risen more than 100 per cent while wages remain at pre-SAP levels, and purchasing power has declined more than tenfold as the following table 6.1 shows. In fact, the devaluation of the national currency made foreign exchange unaffordable to local importers, thereby exacerbating the commodity scarcity problems nationwide.

Table 6.1

Combined Urban and Rural State Consumer Price Index. (Base Period: September 1985 = 100)

State	Dec.1989		Nov.1990		Dec.1990	
	Food	All Items	Food	All Items	Food	All Items
Akwa	333.3	286.5	333.7	294.3	338.0	297.7
Anambra	307.4	287.2	307.5	307.4	311.6	310.4
Bauchi	295.9	286.1	280.8	282.8	279.5	283.4
Bendel	354.3	309.6	348.4	321.8	351.5	326.8
Benue	398.2	354.7	417.3	383.5	331.4	323.1

Table 6.1 (con't)

State	Dec.1989		Nov.1990		Dec.1990	
	Food Items	All Items	Food Items	All Items	Food Items	All Items
Borno	248.2	250.1	299.0	297.2	301.5	299.3
Cross R.	298.2	278.7	267.7	270.0	276.8	273.2
Gongola	284.7	267.3	331.7	305.5	338.7	309.0
Imo	441.6	366.8	323.4	297.0	342.4	310.9
Kaduna	264.6	244.2	306.2	274.7	297.9	274.0
Katsina	248.3	269.2	282.0	276.1	275.2	273.0
Kano	204.8	211.3	239.8	237.9	234.6	236.0
Kwara	426.1	376.8	361.7	329.8	375.0	342.2
Lagos	294.2	288.9	297.1	308.2	306.2	318.7
Niger	249.9	252.6	250.5	259.2	244.4	257.7
Ogun	353.3	318.6	323.2	295.3	321.6	296.0
Ondo	337.9	296.6	351.3	312.2	361.3	320.5
Oyo	299.1	292.0	307.2	309.3	298.7	305.9
Plateua	241.3	245.1	250.6	252.3	271.4	267.5
Rivers	330.8	304.3	368.9	357.7	399.7	379.5
Sokoto	244.9	242.5	256.3	245.1	279.7	264.1

Source: Federal Office of Statistics. Reproduced from the United Bank for Africa's Monthly Business and Economic Digest, Vol.14, No.3 March 1991, p.8.

"Democratization" and Repression

The general belief is that the economic crisis of 1979-1983 under the Shagari regime disrupted the national economy. But it also restricted the potential for accumulation by international capital within Nigeria. Neither the civilian Shagari regime nor the seven-month military regime of Buhari-Idiaghon which followed it were willing to embrace the SAP. Therefore, international capital and its allies threw their support to the December 1983 coup led by Major General Buhari coup, and later, the coup of August 1984 that brought General Ibrahim Babangida (Badru, and Turner 1984).

In retrospect, the Nigerian political debate (1986-1987) around a transition to democracy was in part a political maneuver on the part of the military to divert civilian attention from the economic effects of the SAP. While the debate was taking place, the Babangida regime moved to reorganize the repressive apparatus of the state. Within a short period of time, Babangida increased the military's capability to deal with popular resentments and resistance, which the adoption of the SAP was anticipated to produce.

The April 22, 1990 coup attempt by young officers against the now hopelessly dictatorial regime of Babangida, can be seen as the only concerted effort, since 1986, to force Babangida out of office and to redress the negative impact of the program on the general population, especially the poor. The pressure on the military, by the IMF, to quickly complete the execution of the unpopular Structural Adjustment Program also forced the government to take drastic action against middle class intellectuals and workers who had warned the government that what the program was doing was destroying the fabric of social and economic life. It thus became easy for the military to identify university professor and students who were bold enough to speak against the program as enemies of the state and supporters of coup plotters. The coup became a catch word for the government to clamp down on the opposition movement as illustrated below.

By the beginning of 1990, the Nigerian currency, the naira, was drastically devalued from five to fifteen to the U.S. dollar. By 1992, it had fallen to 25 to one U.S. dollar. The IMF had demanded this extreme devaluation as a condition of any further assistance. In March 1992, the IMF required the Nigerian government to abolish the Foreign Exchange Market (Forex), which was riddled with corruption. For instance, multinational corporations and some elements of the Nigerian bourgeoisie purchased dollars at the low, controlled, rate of one to seven; but then resold the dollars at a rate of one to twenty-five on the parallel market. This practice undermined the purpose of Forex, which was, in part, to provide Nigerian industrialists with foreign exchange essential for the importation of crucial inputs.

The closure of Forex spelled the end of any initiative by the national bourgeoisie for productive investment, because now, they have to go to the parallel market where they must pay twenty five naira for one U.S. dollar or forty four naira for one pound sterling. The naira is currently fixed at eighty four naira to one US dollar. The IMF policies for currency exchange (one point of the nine-point program of the SAP) have thus reduced the players on the investment playing ground exclusively to international firms.

Case Studies of State Repression

Between 1985 and 1992, repression of political opponents of the military intensified. The repression was aimed at civil society, notably such middle-class organizations as the Lawyers' Union, civil liberties organizations, women's organizations, and student unions. In early May 1990, several members of these organizations were picked up by the military, which accused them of supporting the attempted coup of April 22. In the course of gathering data for this book, some of these human rights activists were interviewed, and excerpts from those interviews are documented below. These individuals have, at one time or the other, been incarcerated, abducted, or put under constant surveillance by the state security services. Three case studies have been documented here to show the severity of political condition in Nigeria today.

The interviews focus on three activists who, over the years, have been engaged in the campaign for the restoration of the democratic process in a country that has been ruled for the past twenty-three years by the military. Those interviewed included union leaders, human rights lawyers, and members of the intellectual community. As it turned out, some of the union leaders who had, through correspondence, previously agreed to take part in this project were not available because they had been locked up by the military following the failed coup of April 22, 1990.

Among those interviewed for this book were two university professors who had just been released from maximum security prisons. They had been condemned to death by the

Armed Forces Ruling Council (AFRC), which had accused them of supporting the April 22nd coup. Two human rights activists, who had narrowly escaped from an attempted abduction by government agents days before interview also participated. Efforts were made my this author to include government officials in these interviews but to no avail. The interview arranged with the president, General Ibrahim Babangida, was cancelled at the last minute because, the president did not approve of the contents of our questionnaire.

Case 1: The Killing of a Journalist

In the fall of 1986, a Nigerian journalist was killed by a powerful explosion in his home in Lagos. The journalist, Dele Giwa, was apparently sent a parcel bomb by state security agents acting on instruction from the president. Chief Gani Fawehinmi took on the case of the assassination of the journalist. When interviewed, the lawyer reported that he had been sent to prison and military detention centers six times for venturing to prosecute the security agents involved in the murder of the journalist. Mr. Fawehinmi recast the events that led to the death of the journalist, and his own personal experience with state security agents in the interview excerpt below:

> My client (Dele Giwa) received a parcel bomb from the President's office, and according to his wife, when he saw the stamp on the parcel he said 'this must be from the president.' As soon as he opened the parcel, there was a huge explosion, and Dele was killed instantly. The wife recollected that the previous day, Dele had received a phone call from Dodan Barracks (the seat of the military government), and on the line was the chief security officer to the President, Mr Togun, telling Dele Giwa that the 'problem' he had with the government has been resolved. He (Mr. Togun) then told Dele that he should expect an invitation from the President the following day. What arrived the following day was the parcel bomb. (Interview, Lagos, August,1992)

Once Fawehinmi set in motion the judicial procedure to prosecute the security officers involved in the case, he found out that the military government would not allow the due process of justice to take its course. According to the lawyer, shortly after the case was brought to court, the military promulgated Decree Number 9, which removed the president, state military governors, and other top government officials from the jurisdiction of the civilian courts. In addition, the military also reinstated Decree Number 2 of 1983, which made jail terms mandatory for journalists who publish information that it regarded defamatory to the military administration, even if such information is true. In effect, the military set the stage to forestall any action that might be brought against the security officers involved in the killing of the journalist.

The next surprise, according to the lawyer, was that the case went quickly through the normally slow Nigerian justice system in matter of days. And surprisingly, according to him, the case was dismissed, even though neither of the two security officers charged in the case ever showed up in court. In retaliation against the lawyer for bringing the case to court, the accused officers filed a motion with the High Court in Lagos charging defamation of character, and asking for 6 million naira (then about 2 million U.S. dollars) in monetary compensation.

According to Chief Fawehinmi, before he could defend the lawsuit against him, the judge, on instruction from the military, ruled in favor of the security officers. He recounted his experience following the court decision:

> I was immediately taken to a jail in Gussua some 2,500 kilometres from Lagos. It was a six by six cell with a wooden panel without a roof, in the middle of the Sahara desert. The heat was too much that I had to strip to my underpants. Besides the heat, the government deliberately pumped wild desert scorpions and lizards into my cell which made it impossible to lay on the floor. There were lizards on the walls and floor as well, and I had to share the little food I was given with the lizards. (Interview, op.cit.)

Throughout his incarceration, Mr Fawehinmi suffered several breakdowns, and according to him, a heart problem that had worsened because the prison officials refused to allow him the use of his medication. After six months in prison, his lawyers and other civil liberty organizations, managed to get his appeal to the Court of Appeal where it was immediately thrown out. The lawyer was returned to the same prison where he was made to spend another six months before he was finally released.

As this report was being compiled, Fawehinmi faces numerous criminal and civil charges in federal and state courts. Some of these charges, according to the lawyer, are directly related to his efforts in the Dele Giwa case. Besides these criminal charges, the lawyer faces disciplinary action from the Nigerian Bar Association (NBA), whose conservative leadership has been seeking to strike Gani Fawehinmi's name from the bar list, in effect would make it impossible for him to practice law in Nigeria again. Similarly, the human rights lawyers who took up the case of Gani Fawehinmi have themselves been subjected to all sorts of abuse and intimidations by the state security agents. For instance, Alao Aka-Bashorun, who was formally president of the Nigerian Bar Association, was arrested and detained at the Murtala international airport in Lagos as he was about to board a plane to Colombia where he was to attend the conference of international jurists (State Department's report,1992).

In Mr Bashorun's case, he was removed to a secret military detention center in Lagos where he was questioned for several hours. His international passport was seized and he was placed on order not to travel out of the country, while the military intelligence investigates his human rights activities. Mr. Bashorun has since fled the country for his personal safety. The military continues to hold the passport of Gani Fawehinmi thus preventing him from seeking medical treatment abroad for his heart condition. Several of the human rights lawyers who went to court on behalf of the activists detained under Decree Number 4 were routinely arrested by state security agents. The purpose of this harassment, according to one of the lawyers was to keep them away from future representation.

Case 2:   The Violation of Academic Freedom

Shortly after the failed coup attempt of April 22, 1990, the military blockaded the major universities and began an exercise of seeking out elements the authority described as "subversives". The military has always accused university professors of either being too sympathetic to coup plotters or attempting to incite students against "constituted authority". Indeed, the wave of arrests that followed the attempted coup was not a surprise to the majority of professors. Many professors fled their residences, and those unfortunate enough to remain behind were picked up by military intelligence officers. Two of those professors who were arrested took part in this project.

Professor Toye Olorode and Dr. Idowu Awopetu were outspoken opponents of military rule. The two professors were arrested on May 2, 1990, and scheduled for execution by a military firing squad because of treason charges filed against them. However they got a presidential reprieve and were subsequently released on August 1, 1990. Both Awopetu and Olorode were, at the time of their arrest, professors at the Obafemi Awolowo University (formerly the University of Ife), and both were active members of the Ife Collective, and the Movement Against Second Slavery (MASS). They were released a few days before the interview was conducted. Both had been physically and mentally tortured by their military interrogators. The interview took place at a secret location at the university campus on August 8, 1992. Professor Olorode recounted their arrest:

> Myself and Dr. Awopetu were arrested early morning of May 2 by armed security agents and soldiers. We were taken to the headquarters of the State Security Service (SSS) in Lagos. At the detention center, there were a lot of other people who have been arrested in connection with the coup. They locked us up in a ten

> by twelve room with other eight prisoners. The inter-
> esting thing was that for twenty two days no one told
> us why we were being held. In the detention cell, we
> were forced to draw water to drink from an exposed
> pipe which we also used for cleaning as well. All the
> ten of us in the tiny cell were forced to share a waste
> bucket that was placed close to the exposed pipe. (In-
> terview, Ile-Ife, August,1992)

The professors could not contact their colleagues or families
for several weeks. The university also could not give information to their relatives because of the fear of reprisals from the
military. And, as the professors explained during the interview, many people usually die in detention. In many cases,
relatives of those detained under the emergency decree are
not aware of the whereabouts of their loved ones until they
have been listed as missing persons. Thus for the two professors, the need to make contacts with colleagues became their
major preoccupation. However, they were soon to discover
that it was absolutely impossible to make such contact. Professor Olorode recounted that:

> For twenty two days, I did not see the sky. We were
> only allowed to walk along the corridor that leads to
> nowhere. On June 28, we were taken to another mili-
> tary detention, and yet no one told us why we were
> being detained. It was after we went on hunger strike
> that we were arraigned before a military panel where
> we were told that our arrest was in connection with
> the coup, and on our views on the structural adjust-
> ment program (SAP) which the military adopted as a
> precondition for borrowing money from the Interna-
> tional Monetary Fund. (Interviews op.cited.)

In addition to the physical torture and frequent intimidations,
by prison guards, the appalling conditions in the prison contributed greatly to the rapid deterioration in the professors'
physical and mental conditions. By the time they were released,
both were emaciated to the point that their families could hardly

recognize them. They attributed their physical condition to the poor prison environment and the overcrowding in the prison cells. In a report prepared in 1990 for the U.S. Senate by the State Department, the authors pointed to the conditions in the Nigerian prison system that they considered outrageous by any standard. The report notes that:

> Most cells are filthy, with no toilets or water, and poor ventilation; vermin is rampant. Most long- term prisoners suffer respiratory ailments, and medical care is inadequate. One credible source indicates that pregnant women prisoners may deliver in prison with little medical care or help. Prison born children may remain there for some time, without adequate nutrition or medical attention. (*Country Report on Human Rights Practices For 1990,* p.285).

After the men were in prison for over two months, their families went to the high court seeking their release. According to the professors' account, at the court hearing, they were told that they were being held under Decree Number 2, which allowed the military to detain opponents of the regime for up to six months. In the meantime, families and friends of the professors were also being put under surveillance in a desperate attempt to find incriminating evidence against them, should their case finally go to court.

During the entire duration of their incarceration, the professors were denied access to newspapers and writing materials or books. While the government denied direct involvement in the detention of the two professors, President Ibrahim Babangida made it clear, according to newspaper reports, that no university lecturers would be allowed to "disrupt the economic program" of the military administrators. Dr. Awopetu forcefully drew the connection between the persisting economic crisis (plus the military economic and political agenda) and the intimidation of university professors. During the interview, he noted that:

> Any time the state is in crisis, the government always
> looks for a scapegoat. And those of us in the academy,
> who hold views dissimilar to those of the military, are
> like sitting ducks. Not only the university professors,
> but also workers and students who opposed govern-
> ment economic and social policies, are equally targets
> of government repression once the national economy
> is in crisis. The events of April 22 only gave the mili-
> tary all the excuse it needed to pursue its policy of
> repressing academic freedom and freedom of expres-
> sion. (Awopetu, excerpts from interview, 1992)

After the professors were finally released in August they continued to face harassment from local and national security
agents. For instance, six weeks after their release, the two
professors received a back dated letter from the federal minister of Education, Professor Babatunde Fafunwa, terminating
their appointments. The minister's reason for firing the two
professors was that they had over-stepped their role as teachers, and that "their continuing presence in the civil service is
not in the best interest of the public." Apparently, the minister was acting on instruction from the military junta who saw
academic freedom as a threat to political and economic order.

It is important to note that the professors were released
because state security agents could not present sufficient evidence to prosecute them. It is ironic that the same state would
then turn around and fire them from the academy. However,
on a closer examination, this research discovered that the
firing of the two professors was part of a pattern of academic
control that was set in motion when the military government
decided to implement the SAP.

For instance, in the first week of January, 1990, the government received a $120- million loan from the World Bank
to restructure and revamp the education system. The loan came
with a number of conditions among which were: 1). increased
tuition fees as a means of increasing university revenues, 2). a
rationalization of academic programs aimed at reducing ad-
missions by 15 percent, and 3). removal of excess academic
staff (Liberty, CLO, Vol 1 No.1, June 1990). The eligibility

criteria of the loan, in its third year, will mean that 50 percent of the academic staff in the university system nationwide will lose their jobs. Because of this, opposition to the loan has grown dramatically since the idea was put into effect, and those professors who were bold enough to publicly denounce the loan were seen by the military as "saboteurs", and were often the targets of state repression. Both Professor Olorode and Dr. Awopetu have been vocal opponents of the loan, and their arrest after the coup of April 22, might not be unconnected to the position they took vis-a-vis the "recolonization" of the institutions of higher learning. In fact, professors who were opposed to the loan, and leading officers of the Academic Staff Union had been warned to restrict from condemning the loan. And prior to the time the two professors were arrested, the climate on university campuses in the country was such that serious criticism of government economic policies was a dangerous exercise.

Case 3 : The Abduction of Two Human Rights Lawyers

Since the collapse of the civilian regime of President Shehu Shagari in 1984, middle class opposition to political repression has been gathering momentum. Several human rights organizations were formed mainly by middle class professionals to focus international attention on human rights violations in Nigeria. The leadership of these organizations is made up of lawyers and medical doctors who themselves have been incarcerated, at one time or another, by the military.

The Committee for the Defence Of Human rights in Nigeria (CDHR) was formed by Dr. Beko Ransome Kuti, a medical doctor, whose brother, the famous Nigerian Afro-beat musician, Fela Anikulapo-Kuti, was sent to prison during the regimes of General Olusegeun Obasanjo, and Buhari/Idiagbon. The gross violation of the civil rights of Dr. Beko's brother, and the death of their mother in the hands of Nigerian soldiers, led to the formation of the CDHR. Two other organizations, the Civil Liberty Organization (CLO), and the Association of Democratic Lawyers (ADL) were also formed to rep resent and defend the rights of working class people who could not afford the high litigation fees of Nigerian lawyers.

Since the attempted coup of April 22, the leadership of these organizations has been targeted by state security forces because of their attempts to help families set bail for soldiers connected with the coup. Shortly before my arrival in Lagos for this research, two of these civil rights activists were abducted by armed security officers, and both were driven to the outskirts of Lagos where an attempt to kill them was foiled by sheer luck. The two were Dr. Beni Beko Kuti, the president of CDHR, and Mr. Femi Falana, the president of the Association of Democratic Lawyers. In an interview in Lagos with this author, Mr Falana narrated his experience in the hands of the state security service (SSS) officers thus:

> The security forces came to my house around 4 a.m. in the morning. They informed me that the president wanted to see me. When I demanded to see the invitation from the president, the officers pulled out a faked warrant and told me that I was under arrest. The next thing I knew was that I was bundled into a security van and driven out of Lagos to Epe some forty five kilometres from Lagos. They stopped, and two of the security men came out of the van. They led me into the bush where I was viciously beaten. One of them poured some powdery substance on my body and left me for dead. (Interview, 1992)

The lawyer was rescued by villagers who found him unconscious. He was later taken to the village where they arranged for him to travel back to Lagos. While Mr Falana was driven northeast of Lagos, Dr . Beni Beko Kuti, president of CDHR, was driven southwest, in the opposite direction. In my interview with Dr. Beko in Lagos he confirmed that he shared a similar experience with Mr Falana, except that his captors tried to force a poisoned capsule down his throat. He was rescued by passengers in a commercial vehicle who saw what the soldiers were doing to him. The use of contaminated capsules to kill political opponents, is one way of concealing evidence that those opponents had died in the hands of security agents. Since this interview was carried out, the human rights situation in Nigeria has deteriorated sharply. Many of the activists I interviewed, in the course of this research, have either been killed or incarcerated. However, the momentum generated by their resistance has since given rise to a strong democracy movement which we discuss in the proceeding chapter.

Chapter 7

Transition to Democratic Rule?

The desire on the part of the military to concede to the idea of transfer of power to civilians was, in part, necessitated by pressure from international capital as was argued in the previous chapter. However, the persistence of the political and economic crisis during 1979-1983 under the Shagari regime, and the widespread corruption that riddled his government, not only disrupted the national economy, but had also restricted the potential for accumulation by international capital within Nigeria.

The military interruption was seen as a period to stabilize the political space and maintain some modicum of order in an extremely fragmented economic environment. Neither the civilian regime of President Shagari's nor the interim populist military regime of Buhari-Idiagbon was willing to go so far as to embrace the Structural Adjustment Program proposed by the IMF. Therefore, international monopoly capital and its allies threw their support to the coup led by General Ibrahim Babangida (Turner and Badru,1984). But Babangida was careful enough not to reveal his willingness to implement the SAP and the new autocratic rule that was to follow. Instead, Babangida signalled his intention to usher in a new era of civilian rule by announcing a timetable for a smooth transition to democratic rule.

The political debate during 1986 and 1987 over the transition to democracy was in part a political maneuver on the part of the military to divert civilian attention from the economic effects of the SAP. While the debate was taking place,

Babangida moved to reorganize the repressive institutions of the state. Within a short period of time, Babangida increased the capability of the military to deal with the popular resentments which the SAP was anticipated to generate.

In April 22, 1990 there was a coup attempt by young officers against the now hopelessly dictatorial regime of Babangida. This coup can be seen as the only concerted effort, since 1986, to force Babangida out of office, and to redress the social and economic crisis precipitated by the adoption of the SAP. The coup lasted for two days with the leaders of the coup proposing to expel the northern half of the federation. However, the ethnic background of the coup makers and their incoherent rhetoric were soon to give General Babangida a chance to regroup his forces against the belligerent young officers who were mainly from the southern and middle sections of the country.

The coup itself was rather complicated because of the involvement of a wealthy Nigerian businessman, Great Ogoru, who was said to have singlehandedly financed the enterprise. The leader of the coup, Major Salibar Mukoro, told this author that he and several southern officers were disgruntled over promotional opportunities for southern officers and the increasing domination of military and government contracts by northern businessmen. According Major Mukoro, Great Ogboru, who come from the same local government area as himself, were both disillusioned by the economic, social and political trends in the country, which both perceived, marginalized their ethnic group.

Ogboru, especially, had problems with General Babangida, whom he believed, was deliberately excluding southern businessmen and women from partaking in the booty of the state. With his personal grudge with the Hausa dominated military echelon, and his extreme dislike of the then army chief of staff, Major General Abacha, Mukoro's chance meeting with Great Ogboru in Lagos early in 1989, was to lay the basis for the failed coup. Indeed, Major Dimka, who took the fall for the coup, and later executed by firing squad, according to Mukoro's account, was not originally involved in the planning of the coup. According to him, Major Dimka was brought in at the last minute so that the plotters will not be seen as selfish and ethnocentric southern officers.

The failure of the coup, as it turned out, gave Babangida the opportunity to extend state repression of political opponents while at the same time speeding up the execution of the SAP. Several of the coup officers were hurriedly tried and executed in order to pre-empt any international call for leniency. Indeed, Babangida's friend and right hand man, Major General Vatsa was one of numerous officers who were secretly executed. The severity of the punishment was simply to signal to ambitious military officers that the Armed Forces Ruling Council would not tolerate any diversion form the full implementation of the SAP.

The Political Debate

When Babangida took over power on August 27, 1985, he promised to return the country to civil rule within six months. Shortly after, he announced a transition time table that will usher in democratic government by 1986. As part of his general tactics to remain in power, Babangida orchestrated a national political debate around what kind of constitutional government that will be best suited to the Nigerian situation. The debate was to produce a blue print for a new constitution with inputs coming from all sectors of the Nigerian society. During the debate, the transition time table was moved forward twice for reasons only known to Babangida himself.

At every turn of the national debate on democracy it became clear that the military was manipulating the discussions and steering the debate along lines that it desired. This manipulation of the transition agenda and other confounding forces, especially the biting effects of the structural adjustment program, led to the junior officers' coup attempt of April 1990.

The transition program of the military has been riddled with numerous discrepancies, which made the opponents of the regime suspect that the military was planning for a diarchy type of government. But given the complexities of Nigerian society, particularly middle class suspicion of the military in politics, the idea of diarchy whether openly stated or privately discussed, was not well received. The opposition had also pointed to the fact that, instead of consolidating democratic institutions, the military indeed continued to batter away at these institutions. For example, the middle class questioned the selective voters' registration drive, which is openly biased against women. During the registration drive, many women are only allowed to register after the electoral agents have sought the permission of their husbands. Worse still, many unmarried women, particularly those living in the big cites of Lagos, Kano, Kaduna, and Port Harcourt, were classified as prostitutes, could not register to vote because of the stigma attached to the status of being a prostitute. On top of all this, the voting procedure was changed under the transition guidelines. The traditionally acceptable secret ballot system, was replaced by an odd voting system that requires supporters of candidates to stand behind them for head counts.

These and anomalies were challenged by the opposition on the grounds of being undemocratic. In response, the government accused opponents of attempting to torpedo the transition process. President, Augustus Aihikhomu, just fell short of labelling the opponents of the military transition program as foreign agents in a press conference, thus:

> It is easy for them to point accusing fingers on people, but have we ever asked in this country how these so called self-styled humanists organizations are funded? Who are their backers; their particular interest in society? Today, we are fighting people responsible for illicit dealing in drugs, rapists, people who want to turn the society into a jungle, but the so-called human rights organizations in this country have interest to defend the rights of these enemies of society more than anything else. (*Africa Watch, Newsletter*, Vol.4, No.5, p.10)

In fact, the Vice-President provided no credible evidence to support this sort of claim. The two main organizations that have continuously fought for the release of imprisoned persons, Civil Liberties Organization and the Association of Democratic Lawyers, have restricted their efforts, in the main, to victims of the attempted coup of April 22, 1990, and to others whose activities have been politically oriented.

The Bungled Transition

At the last minute in the transition agenda, the military decided to annul the process altogether. In early 1992, the AFRC annulled the results of the presidential primaries, banning all the twenty three candidates who took part in the election. The process to halt presidential elections started when President Babangida personally invited two wealthy Muslim businessmen to lead the two main political political parties, the National Republican Convention (NRC) and the Social Democratic Party (SDP). In the final countdown, Alhaji Bashir Tofa, a northern Muslim ran for the presidency on the platform of the NCR, while a southern Muslim, a benefactor of the current military, Alhaji Moshood Abiola, ran on the SDP platform. Both men are widely known to have strong connections with the military.

In order to sidestep the judicial process, and to tighten its grip on the whole process, the military enacted Decree Number 13, which empowered the National Electoral Commission, and the Transition to Civil Rule Tribunal (TCRT) to annul the election results in the event of any irregularities. The same Decree number 13 also empowered the NEC to ban politicians who had condemned the transition program from taking part in the election (" Africa Watch", 6/93). President Babangida, also moved to placate skeptics and critics alike, who believed that the military had no intention of relinquishing power, by abolishing the Armed Forces Ruling Council (AFRC) in January of 1993. In place of the AFRC, Babangida set up the National Defence and Security Council (NDSC) comprised of the president himself, his wife and their close associates.

In another move, Option A4 was introduced after the cancellation of the 1992 presidential election primaries. The plan called for each of the political parties to select presidential candidates beginning at the ward, local, state, and federal levels. This cumbersome process ensured that only those who had the financial means could participate in the presidential elections. Finally, after the results of the May 28 elections showed that the southern candidate was winning the election, a group that called itself the Association for Better Nigeria went to court to seek an injunction against the further release of election results and also asked the court to annul the election results so far declared. Indeed, the same group, led by a wealthy London based Nigerian businessman, Arthur Nzeribe, had earlier called for Babangida to remain in power "until the year 2,000"' ("Africa Watch", June 1993).

But the decision by Babangida to go along with the court's directives cancelling the elections results showed clearly a contradiction in his handling of the transition program. As we noted earlier on, the president had stated unequivocally that only the NEC and the Transition to Civil Rule Tribunal had jurisdiction on matters relating to the election, and as such, were the only bodies who could suspend the election results. It was this sort of contradiction, and the announcement that the military would not hand over power on August 27, 1993 to an elected president in this case, Moshood Abiola, that confirmed many opponents' fears that the whole transition process had been a gimmick right from the beginning. The president's decision to set up a transition government, which was made up of old cronies, brings into question, the future of a united Nigeria.

Indeed, opposition to Babangida's plan for a diarchy has slowly but steadily increased. In a move for unity, a new movement called the Campaign for Democracy, led by Dr. Beko Ransome-Kuti, was formed by several human rights groups and trade unions to oppose Babangida's evasiveness. After the cancellation of the election results, the group called general strikes across the country, and these strikes, effectively paralyzed the major cities in the country, most especially, Lagos and Ibadan ("New York Times", August 16, 1993). The Campaign for Democracy also promised to step up its call for popular uprising if Abiola was not sworn in as the new president, on August 27, 1993.

But the call for Abiola's presidency raises more questions than it answers. First, Abiola was "elected" through a process which everyone, including leading members of the Campaign for Democracy, believed was unconstitutional and illegal. To call for Abiola to be sworn in would amount to giving legitimacy to an illegitimate process.

Furthermore, Abiola was part of the oligarchy of the Second Republic under President Shagari, which brought the country to its current economic woes. And it was no secret in Nigeria that Abiola accumulated his massive wealth through patronage from successive military administrations, including Babangida's. In addition, Abiola's murky business dealings with the regime of the assassinated General Murtala Muhammed, while he (Abiola) was a high officer of ITT operations in Africa and the Middle East, has to be cleared up. So, before Abiola could command the respect and trust of many Nigerians, he would have a lot of explaining to do.

As we have seen, there is a connection between the global political economy and the military's false democratic transition. The question that we now pose is: What kind of political economic relations would be consistent with a transition to genuine democracy? This would depend completely upon the progressive social forces succeeding the present ruling regime. If such forces were in charge of the state, and were committed to overseeing the development of genuine democracy, specific international, state, and local class dynamics would constitute the necessary basis of the survival of such a brave democratic experiment. In addition, these forces would have to map out a new strategy to cope with and survive the given international political economy.

Finally, since the current military agenda to move to democratic rule has failed to achieve its goals, a new alignment must be forged between actors in the Nigerian political economy and the international arena, especially around crucial trade and finance axes. The supply of inputs for the oil industry, and even more importantly, outlets for crude oil and petroleum products are critical. Possible buyers of Nigerian oil include those societies that are import dependent and have reason to favor barter exchange (due to lack of foreign exchange with which to buy oil or due to embargoes). Clearly, successful oil sales depend very much on independent transportation capacities, which the Nigerian state currently lacks. And given the fact that the attention of the international community is on rebuilding eastern Europe, it follows that the resources available for the developing world, and for Nigeria in particular, are going to continue to diminish. This puts a premium on creating new links with friendly regimes in the third world, with a view to working out new economic and political relationships. This is a difficult challenge given the fact that international capital will still continue to insist on dominating the global economy.

The new order in Nigeria, assuming there is one, could address this through mobilizing the people behind it in order to put up a strong opposition to international capital's effort to forestal the new relationships it is seeking to establish with friendly Third World societies. It is significant that the availability of such a vital input as petroleum could make a crucial difference to progressive forces in other third world societies where a move to genuine democracy is imminent.

The Abacha "Democratic" Intrigues

When Babangida left office in October of 1992 after annulling the popular democratic elections that led to the "election" of Alhaji Moshood Abiola, the stage was set for another intrigue in the transition to democratic rule. The transition government that was put in place served only to allow the military a chance to decide who would continue the military rule. As the opposition had expected, the choice of General Sanni Abacha as the interim minister of defence clearly showed that the military was not really ready to give up political power. So, it was not surprising albeit intriguing, Abacha should singlehandedly usurp power.

Since General Abacha came to power in November of 1993, he has set in motion a new transition agenda to democracy that is to last for three years; a civilian is expected to be sworn in by October 1, 1998. This transition program is hardly different from that of his predecessors, General Babangida. It

soon became clear that Abacha was not ready to deal softly
with the opposition. In order to frighten the opposition, Abacha
has resulted to the use of terror as an instrument of rule. The
Provisional Ruling Council (PRC) that was set up by Abacha
was made up of close allies and cronies and several leading
members of the Babangida regime. The PRC oversees a 32-
member Federal Executive Council (FEC) and rules directly
by draconian decrees. In his more than a year in office, General Abacha has used violence and intimidation against political opponents and human rights activists.

The most brazen violation of human rights by the military
government of General Abacha can be seen most poignantly
in the recent execution of the environmentalist and playwright,
Ken Saro Wiwa and eight of his followers in November of
1995 . Indeed, the execution demonstrates the military's lack
of respect for human life and a complete disdain for international opinion. But the execution of Ken Saro Wiwa should
be placed squarely within the context of the politics surrounding the exploitation of crude petroleum in Nigeria by multinational corporations.

Until his death, Ken Saro Wiwa was the popular leader
of the Movement for the Survival of the Ogoni People
(MOSOP), which has consistently fought against the ecological destruction of the Ogoni land in the oil producing area of
southeast Nigeria. The movement also fought for the recognition of the minority rights of the Ogoni people whose land
and resources have been virtually occupied by foreign corporations in search of profit. Ogoniland is one of the earliest
communities in southeast Nigeria in which oil drilling started
some thirty five-years ago by Shell, the Dutch crude petroleum conglomerate. In fact, the first refinery was established
at Eleme, in the heartland of the Ogoni people.

For thirty five years, Shell and other small oil companies,
have pumped crude petroleum from Ogoniland for a profit of
$30 billon dollars. Currently, Shell makes an annual profit of
$170 million from its operation in this community alone. A
small community of only 400 square miles, comprising 321
peasant villages with a total population of 250,000 peasant

farmers, Ogoniland is home to ninety six oil wells and five big pumping stations ("New York Times", February 13, 1996).

At present, Shell pumps 900,000 barrels a day of crude petroleum from this area out which it pockets 257, 000 barrels, nearly a third, before delivering the rest to the rentier Nigerian state. Despite its oil riches, Ogoniland is the most backward area in Nigeria, and the most ecological polluted of all the oil producing regions (Hutcfull, 1984). Since oil exploration began in the area in early sixties, local fish farming has been totally destroyed while constant crude oil spills have turned the land virtually barren. In addition, ceaseless gas flaring has made, and continues to make, life unbearable especially for farmers whose villages are located next to the flaring stations. Reports of birth deformities, complications during child birth, and abnormally high spontaneous abortion rates, amongst women of childbearing age, are but a few of the serious medical calamities that have befallen this community since Shell started its operation there (Badru, 1984). During one of my visits to the oil producing areas in the early eighties, it was not uncommon to see villagers drawing drinking water from polluted ponds (Badru, 1985). Efforts to get Shell just one water tap in the area were frustrated by Shell officials, who did not see such provision as part of their concerns ("New York Times", op.cited).

Between 1976 and 1980, there were 784 reported incidents of crude oil spills involving 1,336,875 barrels of crude oil with Shell showing very little or no concern over the ecological impact of these spillages on the community. Indeed, Shell is on record as saying that it is not its responsibility to show concern for the environment ("New York Times", February 13, 1996). It has also been reported that Shell pays very little attention to safety standards, especially in the developing countries, where it has its operations, compared to similar operations in Europe and North America. It was this sort of destruction and intransigence on the part of Shell plus their refusal to listen to complaints from villagers that led the Ogoni people to form the Movement for the Survival of Ogoni People (MOSOP) to save its environment and its local fishing economy from total collapse.

MOSOP was formed in 1990 to organize against Shell's reckless disregard for human life in the area. The leadership of the group complained to Shell officials about frequent oil spills that destroyed farms and polluted creeks where the villagers fish. MOSOP also sought dialogue with Shell officials to work out a compensation arrangement to offset the loss of livelihood by peasant farmers in the area of Shell operations. But Shell decided to pay no attention to this initially, peaceful protest. It was as a result of Shell insensitivity to the villagers' demand that led the MOSOP leadership to change its tactics and become more confrontational in the hope that it Shell would change its mind and return to dialogue. The villagers then resorted to destroying Shell installations, cutting pipe lines and harassing chiefs who colluded with Shell officials.

Once Shell discovered that the villagers meant business, it approached the federal government for protection. The military government of General Babangida gave permission to Shell to raise its own police to intimidate the villagers. It also gave Shell the power to order its security guards to shoot, on sight, villagers who ventured near Shell flow stations and other installations. By January 1993, the crisis had come to a head when MOSOP was able to mobilize 100,000 peasant villagers in a huge demonstration against Shell. In the end, several people were injured and at least four traditional chiefs who had collaborated with Shell were killed. MOSOP officials referred to these chiefs as "vultures." This incident set the stage for the wanton destruction of the Ogoniland by the Nigerian military leadership.

In the meantime, Shell had moved its staff from all its Ogoni locations as a result of the villagers' protest. As this action was costing the government to lose oil revenue from Shell, it decided to do something about it. By May of 1994, the government decided to raze the Ogoni villages to the ground in the hope that this would encourage Shell to come back and resume its operation. For several days, the military and the "kill-and-go-police" rampaged the area killing and burning houses to the ground and raping women. According to MOSOP officials 2,000 villagers were killed, many of whom were fire bombed in their homes by the occupying federal soldiers. Shortly after this, the government detained the leaders of MOSOP and charged them with the death of the four chiefs.

Despite the contradictory evidence of state prosecutors, and in spite of the fact that many of the witnesses confessed that they have been paid by government agents to lie on the witness stand, Ken Saro Wiwa, the undisputed leader of the movement, and eight of his lieutenants were convicted of murder and treason and were sentenced to die by hanging. The sentence was carried out on the early morning of November 10, in spite of international clemency pleas to have the death sentences commuted. At least twenty-nine other members of MOSOP are awaiting trial on the same trumped up charges. Several MOSOP leaders have fled the country to neighboring countries, and some of its top leaders are currently seeking political asylum in Britain.

What these cases of gross abuse demonstrate clearly is the extent to which the Nigerian state will go in providing the sort of political climate necessary for international capital to operate without hindrance from internal social classes. The idea that international capital can operate in dependent formations such as Nigeria, where poverty is so widespread and state structures so weak, without resorting to some form of state-sponsored violence is yet to be proven right. Those western liberals and petit bourgeois intellectuals who have been advocating democratic reforms in the periphery, ignore the fact that such reforms are incompatible with global capitalist accumulation. In the first place, multinational corporations, operating in the periphery of the world economy, do not pretend to go there to deliver social services or to help the poor. They are there primarily to make money, often blood money. As one Shell official told the "New York Times" reporter in London, shortly after the execution of Ken Saro Wiwa on November 10, 1995, "We can offer advice and we can point out the consequences of an action...But we do not lecture or try to give orders because we do not interfere in politics and government." (New York Times, Feb. 13, 1996). This is clearly double talk considering the fact that it was Shell who initiated the wanton destruction of lives, properties, and livelihood in Ogoniland.

The West must share responsibility with the Nigerian state for this execution. Currently, 41.4 percent of Nigerian crude goes to the United States, making Nigeria the second largest exporter of the highest grade of crude to the U.S. Other western democracies enjoying oil imports from Nigeria include France (8.6 percent), Spain (9.3 percent), Netherlands (5.7 percent), and Canada (4.1 percent). It is the duty of these nations, atleast morally, to put pressure on the Nigerian government to stop the open season on killings of its own people.

Given the current pronouncements of these superpowers, it seems that they would rather get cheap petroleum at whatever cost. That is perhaps the saddest commentary on the twentieth century. In a recent report by the US State department on human rights violations in Nigeria since Abacha came to power, several other cases of extra-judicial killings were documented; victims include journalists, professors, union leaders, and virtually any group within the society that holds views dissimilar to those of the ruling junta. The authors of the report were at pains to describe the deterioration of the civil political climate in the country, thus:

> General Abacha's government relied regularly on arbitrary detention and mass arrest of its many critics... Security forces use excessive force to combat a growing wave of violent crime, killing and wounding a number persons, including innocent civilians. Police tortured and beat detainees, and prison conditions remained life threatening; many prisoners died in custody. Citizens do not have the rights to change their government. To continue its hold on power, the regime enacted or extended a series of harsh decrees restricting press freedom and civil liberties which, like other military decrees, contained clauses prohibiting judicial review of any government action. (*U.S. Department of State Report on Human Rights in Nigeria*, 1995, p.1-2)

International opposition to Abacha's regime has intensified through the combined efforts of environmentalists in Europe and several African American organizations in the United States. In order to placate this international opposition, General Abacha has announced a new three-year transition agenda that will supposedly lead to civilian rule. In the meantime, the military continues to maintain its hold on power, partly through the unwavering support of international capital.

Chapter 8

Democratic Front Against the Military Dictatorship

The slow pace at which concerted opposition to the various military dictatorships in Nigeria was developed reflects the lack of cohesiveness of the civil society. Indeed, meaningful opposition to the military regime of General Abacha did not pick up momentum until the annulment of the June 12, 1993 elections, during which the southern multimillionaire, Moshood Abiola, was presumed to have won a popular mandate. Ironically, the so called June mandate became the rallying point for all the opposition forces who now organize under of the umbrella the United Democratic Front. However, it would be wrong to claim that there has been very little opposition to the military since that would deny authenticity to various battles that have been waged against the military junta since 1976.

The Students' Movement

The most consistent opposition to military rule has come from the Nigerian students' movement, which through its mass based organizations, continues to seek the ouster of the military from political power. Beginning in 1976, during the "Ali Must Go" demonstrations, Nigerian students have taken the revolutionary leadership of defining a political platform that challenges the legitimacy of military rule. It was this platform that is being seized upon by the numerous democratic organizations in Nigeria today.

The "Ali Must Go" campaign marked a watershed in Nigeria politics. The campaign was sparred on by the ruthless massacre of innocent Nigerian students at one of the premier institutions of higher learning in the country-the University of Ibadan. Ever since the Ibadan massacre, the Nigerian university campuses have become political battle grounds which has resulted in the senseless massacre of thousands of future leaders. In fact, the first failed coup against the civilian government of Tafawa Balewa in early 1966 drew its inspirations and leadership from dedicated students who had attended the university. In his book, *Why We Struck*, Major Adegboyega, one of the 1966 coup leaders, described in great detail how the idea of the coup and of a socialist Nigeria had been formed while he was a student at the University of Ibadan.

By 1976, the analysis of the Nigerian crisis by the student movement had changed from one centered on ethnicity to one of class. Indeed, the decision by the General Obasanjo's regime to raise school fees across the board was seen by the student leadership as a mean spirited attack on the working class. By increasing school fees and withdrawing state stipends to poor students, the students believe that the Nigerian state embarking upon a plan to make higher education available only to the children of the rich and powerful. Based on this analysis, the students called a strike to protest the increased school fees in addition and to ask the military to relinquish power to the people.

The military responded to the students' protest by sending the army and the "kill and go" police squad to barricade the campus; by the end of it all, one of the students was killed. As the news of the death of the student, Adepeju, became general knowledge, students across the country joined in the struggle for justice, and it was this that later gave impetus to the "Ali Must Go" movement, which today has been the basic rallying point for the Nigerian students' movement nationwide. The slogan "Ali Must Go" was derived from the name of the minister of education at the time, Colonel Muhamed Ali, a very brutal military administrator.

Since the killing of the student, Adepeju, at Ibadan in 1976, the military has perpetrated even more heinous crimes against Nigerian students. In early June of 1985, the military and the anti-riot police invaded the University of Port Harcourt purportedly to break up a secret meeting of the National Association of Nigerian Students (NANS), which at the time was proscribed by the military government of General Babangida. At the end of it all many students were dragged out of their hostels and beaten up. Several female students were reportedly raped and brutalized by armed police and anti-riots officers. In all, 400 students were arrested and taken to Port Harcourt police cells, facilities that could only take twenty detainees at a time. Professors who were suspected of being too sympathetic to the students' cause were harassed or threatened with dismissal.

In May of 1986, the military invaded the northern University of Ahmadu Bello in the northern city of Zaria. The invasion was precipitated by the students' demand that their vice-chancellor, Professor Ango Abdullahi, be removed for corrupt practices, ineptness, and for interfering unnecessarily in the students union affairs. The students also denounced the government's Structural Adjustment Program. The security forces that were dispatched to quell the demonstrations massacred twenty students, one of whom was a female student who had gone to the balcony of her dormitory to see what was going on. She was shot in the head. The following day, the anti-riot police moved to the campuses of Kaduna Polytechnic, the University of Benin, Obafemi Awolowo University, and the University of Lagos, where students had gathered for solidarity marches for those students killed at Ahmadu Bello University.

A number of students were killed during four days of a killing orgy by the security forces. While the government did not give the exact numbers of students killed, many national newspapers estimated that there were between 20 and 400 were casualties of the massacre. During 1987, there was very little or no activity from the Nigerian students' movement partly because General Ibrahim had instituted a rather bogus transition agenda program, which was supposed to transfer power to the civilian elite in 1990, a date that he later changed to 1993. However, in May of 1988, the university campuses erupted once again. By this time the SAP was biting hard, and the decision of the government to raise fuel prices led to nationwide riots. In the early morning of May 1988, students in thirty three campuses of the Nigerian higher education system confronted the anti-riot police who fired indiscriminately on unarmed students. Several students were killed nationwide. ("West Africa", May 2, 1988 and January 16, 1989).

By early 1989, a new set of riots had broken out at the universities in Lagos, Ibadan, Ife, and Benin. The students were demonstrating against the policies of the World Bank and IMF and when the police and the army besieged those campuses at least six students were killed. However, this riot achieved its main objective, namely drawing the attention of the military leadership to the hardship brought on the masses by the SAP. In fact, at the end of the riots, the government of Babangida agreed to what was described as a "SAP Relief Package." The package included short term measures to combat inflation, the establishment of a mass transit system for workers, the setting up of peoples' banks, and a review of the minimum wage. From 1990 up to the time of this writing, numerous demonstrations against the government by the students have been brutally repressed resulting in deaths, and general mayhem.

Clearly, Nigerian students have played, and continue to play, an important role in terms of the search for democratic reform and good government. The impact this has made on the politics of the military can hardly be underestimated, more important is the fact that it was the students' courage in defying the brutality of the Nigerian military that allowed for the current waves of opposition to the military under the umbrella of the United Democratic Front of Nigeria, which now claims the leadership of the struggle. But the point that should be made is that had the Nigerian intellectuals been less arrogant, they could have found a natural ally in the students' movement. But because of the colonial mentality that imposes an artificial distinction between the university professor and students, the struggle to transform the neocolonial State was undoubtedly hampered. At the peak of the struggle in 1986, when the National Association of Nigerian Students (NANS) proposed a common platform to take on the military with the Academic Staff Union of Universities (ASUU), the professors' union- the leadership of ASUU either dismissed the idea as inappropriate or simply ignored it. If the agreement had happened, the struggle would most certainly have taken a different route.

The United Democratic Front of Nigeria

As emphasized above, the belatedness of the different opposition forces in Nigeria to unite in confronting the military may be due partly to ideological differences and to the divisiveness of ethnic politicking. The belated decision to form the United Democratic Front was partly due to pressure form the private pro-democracy organizations in South Africa and from the Norwegian government. Both the Norwegian government and President Mandela of South Africa were particularly enraged by the senseless execution of the environmentalist and playwright, Ken Saro Wiwa and eight of his followers, in the Movement for the liberation of the Ogoni People (MOSOP), in November of 1994. The execution had outraged the entire world.

The United Democratic Front of Nigeria (UDFN) was officially formed in Oslo, Norway, during a meeting held March 29-31, 1996. The facilitator of the conference was Wole Soyinka, the playwright and Nobel laureate. The UDFN was formed out of thirteen different civil and human rights organizations some of them operating from North America, Europe, and South Africa. Those sending delegates to the Oslo conference included; Action Group for Democracy (AGD), African Democratic League (ADL), Campaign for Democracy (CD), Coalition for Democratic Awareness (CDA), Democratic Alternatives (DA), National Alliance for Democracy (NAD), National Democratic Alliance Committee (NDAC), National Democratic Coalition (NADECO), National Freedon Foundation (NFF), Nigerian Democratic Movement (NDM), National Liberation Council of Nigeria

(NALICON), New Nigerian Forum (NNF), and the Nigerian Liberation Group (NLG). Of the thirteen organizations only three or so of them have reputations inside and outside of Nigeria. The most noted is the Campaign for Democracy (CD) whose leader, Dr. Beko Ransome Kuti, was currently serving time in jail on trumped up charges by the military.

Both the Campaign for Democracy, and its legal wing, the Association of Nigerian Democratic Lawyers, under the leadership of Femi Falana (also incarcerated), have consistently challenged the legitimacy of military rule. Wole Soyinka's entry into the Nigerian liberation movement was very puzzling to a lot of people because of his previous collaboration with the regime of General Ibrahim Babangida. In fact, Soyinka was the director of road safety corps under General Babangida; a position he left under some very bizarre circumstances. However, many who attended the conference saw Soyinka's involvement as important because of the international reputation and recognition that he currently enjoys.

Indeed, it is difficulty to ascertain what unites these groups except for the desire to get rid of the military regime and the reaffirmation of the June 12, 1992 process. The delegates attending the conference formally issued a statement that looks like a programmatic declaration. It declared itself the legitimate opposition to the government of Nigeria and characterized itself as the "Government of National Unity". The UDFN proclamations are as follows:

> 1. We reject in its entirety the three- year transition program of the Abacha dictatorship in Nigeria;
> 2. We reject any actions including the creation of states and the conduction of elections under the illegal Abacha regime shall be null and void;
> 3. The only moral, just and lasting solution to the Nigerian crisis is respect for the mandate of the Nigerian people as expressed in the elections prior to and including June 12, 1993, presidential elections;
> 4. We appeal to all people of conscience all over the world to insist on respect for the will of the people of Nigeria as expressed in the elections prior to and in-

cluding the presidential elections of June 12, 1993;

5. We call on the Nigerians at home to boycott any new elections and to take measures to establish parallel zones of authority at local levels to deny any legitimacy to the Abacha's regime;

6. We demand that all political prisoners in Nigeria be released immediately and without conditions, and also that president- elect, M.K.O Abiola be released to form a broad-based Government of National Unity;

7. We call on the international community to impose oil embargo and full economic, cultural and sporting isolation on Nigeria until democracy is restored;

8. We call on all governments, the UN, OAU, EU and non-governmental organizations to desist from giving the Abacha dictatorship any semblance of legitimacy by a). Not providing any financial, logistic or other support for Abacha's illegal elections; b). Not sending any observers to his shabolic elections;

9. We strongly advise all governments, the World Bank, the International Monetary Fund and other international financial institutions not to negotiate any further debt rescheduling or grant any new loans to the Abacha regime, as the future legitimate government will not be compelled to honor such agreements;

10. We request all governments to freeze all the assets of members of the military junta and their civilian collaborators. (UDFN declaration, Oslo, Norway, March 31st, 1996)

These proclamations contain hardly any strategy for achieving political power nor do they discuss the form of the future government it hopes to establish after gaining political power. As Soyinka himself observes, in his speech to the assembly of delegates, the various organizations came together as a matter of convenience. There is no commitment to any single ideological position, and their vision of a future Nigeria is as blurry as that of the military they are planning to displace. In his speech to the assembly titled "Towards a Sustainable Vision of Nigeria.", Soyinka outlined the reasons that brought all the groups together:

> I believe that we have agreed to assemble here because we can neither understand nor accept the contradictory motions of the political class, its collaborationist approach with those who have placed our people under the most brutal subjugation in our history as Nigerians, as earlier defined ...   Our task here is not to produce an agreement in all details of strategy, but we shall not leave without a definite plan of action, one that is time specific. We do not intend, in a mere two days to weld together differing philosophies and the visions of participating groups, yet we are duty bound to create a unified body for democratic forces of the nation. We are obliged to search out what each group does best, so that we can lunch the new organization on its task of assigning responsibilities that correspond to their past records and future potential... (UDF declaration, Oslo, Norway. pp.1-3)

False Unity

Soyinka's address to the assembly of delegates expresses clearly the precariousness of the opposition's unity against the military junta in Nigeria. The ideological diversity of the UDFN, ranging from the populist party platform of the NADECO to the liberalism of the CD, reflects the confusion within Nigerian opposition circles. This confusion has arisen out of a particular analysis of the Nigerian neocolonial state on the one hand, and on the other, the particularism of the interpretation of the uniqueness of the Nigerian crisis in general. Such confusion only allows for the development of a culture of apathy which the military oligarchy continues to exploit.

For the members of the CD, the Nigerian state is only an aberration to the extent to which its leadership is corrupt. Therefore, fixing the crisis of the state, and by inference, of the civil society, requires the removal of bad leaders through democratic reform. While the CD and NADECO insist that their support of the June 12, 1993 election is based on moral principles, they ignore the fact that the whole electoral process that led to the election of the multimillionaire, Moshood Abiola was a fraud right from the beginning. Chief Abiola himself knew very clearly the sort of risk he was taking when he was singlehandedly picked by General Babangida to lead the Social Democratic Party of Nigeria (SDPN), a party of which he was never a member.

In fact, Abiola's commitment to democracy and justice, in a new democratic Nigeria, is very dubious to say the least. Abiola's decision to run on the platform of the SDPN was largely based on personal ambition and not a commitment to a vision of a new Nigeria. As we argue elsewhere in this book, Abiola's record as a politician and a businessman is hardly anything to brag about home about. Hence, to tie the struggle for democratic reform to the June 1993 process was bizarre and politically unwise.

The crisis of the Nigerian state cannot be reduced to the psychology of its leaders, as Soyinka tends to suggest in his address to the assembly of delegates, because to do that is to ignore the structural imperatives that gave rise, and continue to sustain their conduct. While the UDFN demands seem sensible to the majority of Nigerians, by providing a unity platform, where old and discredited politicians play dominant roles reveals the lack of ideological clarity of UDFN. By aligning itself so closely with the remnants of the politically disgraced oligarchy of the First and Second republics, the UDFN leadership simply exposes its own opportunism. It is simply idiosyncratic, and a wrong political choice, to form a revolutionary platform with the enemies of the past in the name of getting rid of the military. The historical experience of other states in Africa, for example Zimbabwe, where revolutionary compromises were made in the name of national unity, supports this point. Certainly, the UDFN builds has built upon itself a false platform that can hardly carry Nigeria as state, and Nigerians as one people, to the next millennium.

The crisis of the Nigerian state must be understood in terms of its structural relationships, most especially, the rela-

tionship of the state to internal social classes and to its relation to the contradictions and crisis of accumulation. These
two essential contradictions determine the particular character and specificity of the Nigerian class struggle both in relation to the internal accumulation process and its overall relation to international capital. The military emerges as the only
institution that international capital can trust in maintaining
order and stability.

The collapse of the First and Second Republics, both
equally built on false foundations, is symptomatic of this general pattern of a contradiction riddled accumulation process
and the persistence of the crisis of the civil society. A genuine
platform to resolve this crisis cannot be built on formulas of
class compromises, because it has been proven, beyond a
shadow of doubt, that such compromises can only secure and
reinforce the economic interest of the most powerful stratum
in the society. It is within this context that the UDFN's support for the outcome of the June 12, 1993 elections, is plainly
wrong and is a gross underestimation of the power of the old
elites whose economic interests are closely linked to those of
the military oligarchy.

The challenge that the military poses, on the civil society,
should be understood in class terms, and be addressed as such.
The peculiar nature of the economy itself complicates the complexity of the class struggle resulting in a tendency to confuse
struggles at the level of the economic with the political. Thus,
by prioritizing the struggle at the level of the political, the
democracy crowd ignores the crucial contradiction at the level
of the economic. By assuming that getting rid of the military
would automatically guarantee the end of class struggle itself
amounts to crude populism.

What the democracy crowd refuses to do is analyze the
class character of the June 12, 1993 election and see whose
class interest is at stake. Affirming Abiola's right to the presidency is synonymous to rubber stamping the political supremacy of the class he represents, which, in this case, is
the class of the exploiter. The campaign for democratization
must include both a political and economic agenda, most especially the question of the subordinate relationship of the

Nigerian state to both internal and foreign exploiters. Thus, by combining political demands with economic ones, the opposition would have no choice but to produce a platform or program for transforming the entire neocolonial social formation. Needless to say, the military itself is one visible form of the power of the exploiting class, both domestic and foreign; and getting rid of the current junta would add very little to a broader agenda of displacing the hegemony of this class.

Chapter 9

Conclusion:
A Prognosis for Nation Building

The inability of the military to ensure a peaceful transition reflects the failure of the political culture and not necessarily a desire on the part of the military to remain in power as some analysts have mistakenly suggested . Therefore, in order to propose a political alternative to the current crisis, we must examine further the historical experience of Nigerians as a diverse people, and also establish whether the liberal democratic model itself is sufficient in transforming the Nigerian neocolonial situation. In this concluding chapter, therefore, this author examines the ways and mechanisms necessary to overcome the burdensome crisis of political transformation. As it has been consistently argued in the previous chapters, the problems of economic transformation in Nigeria is clearly linked to the political process, and that without a solid political base, economic development will probably remain as elusive as ever.

The Context of Liberal Democracy

Liberal democracy has succeeded in the places where it currently flourishes because the social and economic conditions were initiated prior to the institution of participatory democracy. In continental Europe, especially England and France, the development of democratic institutions involved hard fought struggles between the principal major social classes.

In the European situation, participatory democracy was limited to certain classes and property qualifications were used to regulate participation. The majority of the working people, at the beginning of the process, were excluded from participation, and a gradual incorporation of the lower classes into the democratic structures was followed by the development of ideologies that legitimized the political and economic hegemony of the bourgeoisie.

In the meantime, working-class agitation for inclusion in the political process was brutally repressed by the political elites. In 1789, a working class rebellion cumulated in what is now called the French Revolution. The political turmoil that engulfed imperial Russia gave birth to the Bolshevik revolution of 1919. In Kuomitang China, peasant revolts and the Maoist Long March led to the 1949 revolution that brought Chairman Mao to power. In all these cases, these revolutionary situations produced one common goal- which is the political incorporation of the working masses into the political process.

While the French Revolution may have produced the idea of liberty, freedom, and equality, the end result was a long process of subordinating the laboring masses to the political whims of the property elite, whose political vision is what we now call liberal democracy. In the communist roads to building stable political structures, both Stalinism and Maoism achieved a more bizarre form of participatory democracy in which the working masses were subordinated to the whims and caprices of the communist elites. Whichever way we look at it, there is a definite convergence between the bourgeois and the so-called proletarian road to participatory democracy.

The African Situation

But Africa never went through this struggle except for the different struggles against European enslavement and colonization; the social, historical, and economic trajectories that gave rise to western democratic models were essentially lacking. A hundred year of European colonization had left Africa with political structures that are susceptible to authoritarian rule. Thus, the debate over the importation of western type democracy into the African situation often ignores the fact that democracy can never be implanted .

Democratic institutions, whether European or African, have to evolve organically from a particular environment. In this regard, to talk of western democracy in the context of the African situation ignores the fundamental question of its relevance to the African condition. Africans did not go through the War of the Roses, neither did they go through the French Revolution nor the Chinese or Russian revolutions. If this is the case, then what is the class and social basis upon which we are trying to build a liberal democracy? The answer is none. If this is the case, then we need to look for an alternative to western democracy. The first step in doing this is to remember the fact that Africa has its own past and its own history. This history also includes the existence of a fundamental decision-making process, which is as old as the history of human civilization. By ignoring African historical part, especially its systems of governance before European contact, we continue to ignore the essential ingredients that are necessary for building a good and vibrant society.

The history of modern Africa is almost synonymous with the history of colonialism and, as a result, solutions to African problems are often sought in the colonial experience. But this is not to say that African history begins with colonization; it is quite the contrary. It is a well established historical fact, that various European colonial masters supplanted traditional African democratic structures with European political forms that are completely contradictory to the African experience and the African spirit.

This contradiction may explain the persistence of the African crisis. In short, to develop a stable structure for African democracies, Africans must look back beyond colonization and develop a model that will address their particular needs. What is good in the European model must be retained and possibly refined to meet African needs; and what is bad in the African past must be eliminated and replaced with forms that are compatible with human progress. Idolizing the African past is simply not good enough; however, ignoring the successes of the past is tantamount to subscribing to the notion of European supremacy that was popularized during slavery and colonization.

Options for Nigeria's Democracy

In the past thirty years of independence, Nigerians have proposed several options or models of democratic governments that would take cognizance of the problems of ethnicity. The arguments of the proponents became more forceful after the failures of the both British parliamentary system of democracy that was practiced during the First Republic and the American style of government adopted by the infamous civilian regime of Alhaji Shehu Shagari. Both of these models have their historical usefulness and purposes. The British parliamentary system was imposed on the people of Nigeria by the British imperial state, as we argued earlier, to maintain its own economic dominance after independence. The failure of this British style of centrifugal federalism was obvious as Graf observes:

> The sheer size and diversity in Nigeria, particularly after half a century of indirect rule, precluded any total transference of the unitary Westminster model to the ex-colony. The homogenous nature of British society, its consensual political culture and its advance degree of industrialization-the latter achieved partly at the expense of the colonies at the periphery-ensured the 'proper' operation of parliamentary system there. None of these conditions was present in Nigeria. The British, therefore, in consultation with the Nigerian successor elite, determined to superimpose on the Nigerian state, a system of federalism which, like federalist governments elsewhere, would permit a degree of autonomy and scope for self-development of the multiplicity of the sectoral and ethnic groups, while, at the same time, connecting and holding together these pluralist forces in a common set of and conflict regulating institutions, thus binding them in voluntary and

> self-interested association to the central government.
> Federalism, in other words, was the structural expres-
> sion of the notion of 'unity in diversity.' (Graf, 1988,
> p.29)

This notion of "unity in diversity" envisioned by the British colonial power was never realized. Parliamentary democracy and the idea of centrifugal centralism never materialized. Instead, ethnic identity and rabid competition over scarce resources, as we outlined earlier, led to the civil war between the North and South.

The decision to opt for the American presidential system in 1979 was based on the idea that a powerful president could forge the "unity in diversity" the British parliamentary system had failed to achieve. The members of the Constituent Assembly who recommended the American type presidential system thought that a rotational presidency, in a powerful federal state would promote unity and ethnic understanding. But they were wrong.

As we commented earlier, the Second Republic was riddled with the problems of ethnicity as was its predecessor. Graft and corruption were the order of the day, and with government being run on a patronage system, it became clear that the politics of building national unity was to be turned into politics of resource distribution and private accumulation. As Shehu Othman and Garvin Williams succinctly pointed out:

> Politics was a game of winner takes all. Politicians
> used all the resources, constitutional and extra-consti-
> tutional, to gain and maintain control of office. In the
> 1950s politicians were able to compromise on consti-
> tutional issues and on the allocation of revenues among
> regions because all gained access to something, though
> some gained more than others. After independence in
> 1960, they competed for shares of the same, limited
> resources. Negotiators each sought to protect sectional
> gains not to arrive at a solution to common problems.
> (Othman and Williams, 1995)

The class of traders that took over state power during the Second Republic saw the success of the government in terms of how much money and how many contracts it could distribute to the party faithful. Members of the opposition and minority ethnic groups saw the new government as advancing the economic interests of the North using oil resources from the South. Those southern elites and minority peoples who could not get their share of the booty were soon to constitute themselves into a strong opposition bent on bringing the Second Republic down. On the other hand, the class of retired military officers, who had transferred power to the new civilians, were increasingly being marginalized from the process of accumulation. As we argue elsewhere (Turner and Badru, 1985), it was the marginalization of this retired military elite, most of whom have now established themselves as capitalist farmers with stolen state funds, that finally led to the collapse of the Second Republic.

The Confederacy Option

With the collapse of the Second Republic, many politicians, particularly those that were marginalized from the process of accumulation, were now beginning to cast doubt on federalism as a viable option for Nigerian democracy. One of the first politicians to call for a new confederate state was the former governor of Ogun state, Chief Olu Adebanjo, who argued that federalism had only advanced the economic and political advantages of the Hausa-Fulani oligarchy.

In practical terms, confederacy was presumed to recognize the autonomy of each region, and this autonomy would include the freedom to exploit resources under their jurisdiction without the interference of a federal power. Each confederate state of the union would exercise power over everything except defence and foreign policy, which would be managed by the council of a rotating presidium. The council of presidium would be made up of elected representatives from each of the autonomous regions. However, a closer look at the arguments of the proponents of the confederal state reveals several potholes in the road to implementation.

First, there is the question of resource allocation. While this particular issue is not openly stated in the confederacy proposal, one can assume that each state, constituted by ethnic block, would control the resources over its territories. This evidently would contradict the idea of one Nigeria because of the lopsided way in which natural resources are distributed. The North, which covers fifty percent of the total land mass, and with population twice the size of the rest of the country put together, has very few resources to sustain it as a sovereign state. Hence it is no surprise that opposition to confederacy came from northern politicians.

Second, the question of minority groups, and their rights under a confederal state, is even more problematic than the issue of the north/south divide. The land claims of many minority groups, especially the Ogoni people of southeast Nigeria, include most of the crude petroleum the Nigerian state depends on for its operation. It is very clear that the confederacy option would be more popular with minority ethnic groups than the rest of the nation. However, in order to achieve confederal rule, there would need to be a of repeal colonial and postcolonial ordinances and decrees that make natural resources, such as crude petroleum, the property of the federal government. One such ordinance was the 1976 Land Use Decree, which was promulgated under the regime of General Obasanjo in anticipation of future agitation for regional autonomy. Thus it is clear that for some of the reasons outlined above, confederacy is perhaps the most dangerous option because it carries the potential for another civil war.

However, the problem of resource allocation could be resolved, without a doubt, in case the country opts for the concept of autonomous confederal regions, possibly based on the pre-war arrangement. A new formula that allows each region to keep seventy five percent of resources found in its area, while twenty five percent of such resources is submitted to a central fund, will go a long way in solving the problem of resource allocation that lays at the heart of the Nigerian socio-economic, and political crises. In addition to this, all off-shore mineral resources, including but not limited to crude petroleum, will automatically be allocated to the central fund. The central fund will be used to finance smaller autonomous regions that are resource poor. This will definitely solve the minority question since each ethnic minority in each of the autonomous regions will exercise control over resources found in its particular area.

The Diarchy Option

The diarchy option is perhaps the least popular option except in the ranks of the military leadership. The idea of diarchy itself came originally from the desperation of another military despot in the neighboring country of Ghana. In his most unpopular days right before he was executed, General Achampong of Ghana envisioned a form of government in which the civilian and military elites would cooperate in a new government of national unity. The proposition was based on the simple, albeit dogmatic, idea that the military is essentially part of civil society, and therefore, it should have an equal say in the administration of government. Fortunately or unfortunately, General Achampong was unable to outline the mechanics of a diarchy government before he was tied to the stake and shot by the young military officers who overthrew him.

It was during the last desperate days of General Babangida that the idea of diarchy for Nigeria temporarily surfaced before it was buried under the platitudinousness of the national debate. In a diarchy government, the military and the civilian elites would share political power at the state and federal levels. A presidium of military and civilian council will be established at the federal level with a mixed cabinet of politicians and service officers. The same would be replicated at the state levels, except that the council of the presidium would be replaced by a gubernatorial council. The politicians would be allowed to compete for elections at the local level, but the real power would be retained by the gubernatorial executive council that would jointly be presided over by a military officer and a civilian deputy. Since the military would be represented at all levels of governance, according to this model, there would be no need for military coups.

While it is impossible to predict how power sharing between the military elite and the political class would resolve the fundamental contradictions of accumulation and resource allocation, one thing that is clear is that diarchy is more like a collaboratory oligarchial rule than a participatory democracy. But the mutual distrust between the military and political class might itself pose serious problems for international capital who would rather deal with a class that has internal coherence.

The Ideological Option

The position taken in this book is that class compromises between the military oligarchy and the civilian elite, cannot resolve the central contradictions of the Nigerian state. The persisting antagonistic relationship between the elite class and the producing classes are at the heart of the Nigerian crisis. Ethnicity as a political ideology is the creation of the British imperial power, which the political elite whether in the civil society or the military continues to use. Therefore, to resolve the crisis requires a fundamental class reorientation of the Nigerian masses toward a political program of action that is totally devoid of ethnic or religious interventions.

At present, class consciousness amongst the Nigerian masses is oddly very ethnocentric since many see support for ethnic leaders as a vehicle for group advancement. Thus, there is a need to build a new political culture in which clearly defined interests are articulated and political opportunism amongst the political class is exposed. A new agenda for achieving national identity must be set that will involve setting up educational and cultural programs that emphasize this identity as opposed to old ethnically based primordiality. But this can be achieved only by destroying existing colonial structures and redefining the relationship of the Nigerian state to both international capital and the British imperial state, which continues to determine the form and content of Nigerian polity and culture.

In this context, a popular movement for the restoration of African participatory democracy must emerge under the vanguard of the people themselves. Nigerian intellectuals could contribute their talents to this process by doing more in-depth research into the African oral tradition so that they could reconstruct the lost model of African democratic past. This knowledge would assist the people in the process of building a nation that transcends ethnicity.

The obvious problem is, of course, the persisting influence of old ideologies through which the hegemony of traditional oligarchies are maintained. These ideologies come in the form of religious dogmas, particularly in the far north, where Islamic teachings by the mullahs and collaborators have generated subservience in the psyche of their followers, reminiscent of the worst form of feudalism. The new movement must tackle the issues of religiosity amongst the masses by directly exposing the interests of the mullahs and Islamic teachers and their relationships to the feudal oligarchy.

Similarly, in the southwest the traditional power of the chiefs must be challenged and exposed for what it is, and the use of magic and other mythological practices must be denounced. In the old western region, the politics of the sixties and seventies were based on the influence of the political class and the traditional rulers who often deliver the support of their subjects to unscrupulous and corrupt politicians. The new movement for democratic renewal must emphasize political education of the masses and secular discourse must replace old taboos that currently prevail amongst the majority of Nigerians. While it is difficult to see how this can be achieved, it is a feasible program, which with dedication and commitment in the ranks of the new political vanguard, could be achieved within a few years.

In sum, traditional structures must be replaced with new secular ideas. The educational institutions in their current form will need to be replaced, and a new structure must be built that is amenable to the growth of new ideas. The British education structure that was left behind after independence was designed to enslave our peoples minds in much the same way religious ideologies do. This can only be achieved through a radical restructuring of the relations of the masses to the means of production in a direction that ensures fairness, particularly for those who are currently alienated and excluded from the process of distribution.

Indeed, a new social and cultural revolution is a necessary precondition for achieving this goal of building a new society. This revolution must focus on attacking the widespread mentality of material culture, insolence, ego-worshipping, nepotism, graft, corruption, lack of discipline, and all other evils that continue to gnaw on the body of Nigerian society in general. Blaming colonialism and imperialism for Nigerian problems is probably one thing that has prevented us from seeing those internal characteristics in us that continue to reproduce the structure of foreign domination. All negative aspects of the culture must be renounced, while those that are compatible with the sustenance of the social system in all its modern complexities, must be retained.

Postscript

Since General Sanni Abacha seized state power in November of 1993, things have taken a more bizarre turn especially in the increasing numbers of assassinations of political opponents, including the assassination of Mrs. Kudirat Abiola, the wife of the president-elect, Chief Moshood Abiola. Mrs. Abiola was murdered by unknown gunmen, on the street of Lagos, gunmen that opposition leaders believed have connections with the military. In the meantime, there are clear indications that the military ruler, Sanni Abacha, may not want the transition agenda to run its course as was the case with General Babangida, his predecessor.

For instance, shortly after the announcement of the new transition agenda, Abacha introduced even tougher measures to preclude popular participation in the electoral process. One of these is the legal condition that requires all candidates to produce photographs of all their supporters in all the states of the federation. In order to intimidate opposition critical of the transition agenda, the military recently introduced the Transition to Civil Rule Decree that makes anyone "who organizes, plans, encourages, aids, cooperates or conspires with any other person to undermine, prevent or in any way do anything to forestall or prejudice the realization of the political program" liable to automatic five years imprisonment (Richard Joseph, 1996). It is such decrees that make observers doubt Abacha's sincerity to his own proffered willingness to relinquish political power in 1998.

In the event that the transition agenda is not fully realized by its 1998 deadline, there are three possible scenarios. The first scenario is that Abacha may simply refuse to vacate office and remain in power indefinitely in the manner General Mobutu Sese Seko did in Zaire. This is what some political observers have described as the "road to Zaire." Alternatively, Abacha may simply decide to vacate office shortly before the election in 1998 and then put himself up as a presidential candidate of one of the political parties, thereby legitimizing his hold on power like Jerry Rawlings in Ghana. The third scenario is a bloody one which might lead to another civil war. Civil war is the most likely option, especially if one of the Yoruba leaders, Abiola or Obasanjo, dies in prison; a Yoruba led military coup might then lead to such a war.

The first scenario is possible only if the international community, especially western nations with crude oil interests in Nigeria, decide that there is no credible replacement to Abacha among the opposition elements in the prodemocracy movement. In this case, Abacha may decide, with prompting from these western nations, to release Abiola with a promise of granting him some figurehead role as civilian president in a military diarchy government. However, this plan would most likely be rejected by northern senior military officers who are waiting in the wings to replace Abacha in 1998. The degree to which Abacha can resist serious threats from these officers, mainly Hausa/Fulani renegade elements in the army, will largely depend upon how much military assistance he can get from those western powers to repel these officers.

The "road to Accra," is another option opened to Abacha, an option that is presently being encouraged by Abacha's supporters in the north. Like, Jerry Rawlings of Ghana, Abacha may retire from the army and put himself forward as a presidential candidate in a future election. However, this option will represent a difficult option to international capital, which would rather see a limited form of democratization as a means of giving legitimacy to the whole process of accumulation in Nigeria. However, if the economic conditions improve significantly in the meantime, either through the re-evaluation of the currency or the abandonment of key elements of the SAP, then Abacha will most likely be seen by the people as a lesser evil than those who might replace him.

The option of another civil war is very strong, and it is the least considered by many analysts. The war, which would most likely be between the Yoruba and the Hausa-Fulani oligarchy of the north, would most probably come, either because of the possibility of Abiola's death in prison or by perceived marginalization of Yoruba elite from the political process. Another factor that may trigger the war could be the refusal of the north to go with a confederacy arrangement, which many Yoruba of the southwest, currently believe is the best solution to the Nigerian crisis. Since the center of internal accumulation is in the northern part of the country, and with the reality that the north might not survive as an independent state, the war option, similar to the ethnic war of 1967, becomes a very tangible option to the current political impasse.

But the position the Igbos might take in the event of a war is uncertain, and with the balancing acts and ethnic accomodationist position of the Igbo leadership, it is most unlikely that the Igbo would join with the Yoruba in any direct confrontation with the North. Nevertheless, the Igbo could see an advantage in playing a neutral role in any possible conflict between the old West and North, by rejecting the entire north-south divide, and as a result, separately declaring their own independent state along the ethnic boundary of the old Biafra nation. If this were to happen, the country would be thrown into some ethnic violence similar to what is currently going on in Liberia.

What is clear is that Nigeria has not been able to find a solution to the persisting ethnic problems which are, in most part, a result of an artificial boundary, created in 1914 by the British imperial state for its own aggrandizement- a boundary that put culturally and linguistically diverse peoples in one single nationless state. In the end, a Nigeria with many different boundaries, may be the solution to the endless crisis of polity, and ethnicity, in the absence of a socialistic consolidation of state power.

Bibliography

Abrams, P.1989. Historical Sociology. Ithaca, N.Y: Cornel University
    Press.
Academic Freedom and Human Rights in Abuses in Africa. Africa
    Watch Document, London and New York, April,1991.
Achike, O. 1973. Groundwork of Military Law and Rule in Nigeria.
    Enugu: Fourth Dimension.
_____, 1982. Public Administration: A Nigerian and Comparative
    Perspective. London: Longman.
Adamolekeun, L. 1985. The Fall of the Second Republic. Ibadan: Spec-
    trum Books.
Adedeji, A. 1969. "Federalism, Economic Planning and Plan Admin
    istration." NISER Conference Paper.
_____, A. 1989. Towards a Dynamic African Economy. London:
    Zed Press.
Adegboyega, A. 1981. Why We Struck: The Story of the First
    Nigerian Coup. Ibadan Evans.
Adepoju, A. (ed.). 1993. The Impact of Structural Adjustment Pro-
    gram on the Population of Africa. Portsmouth: UNFPA &
    James Currey.+
Afigbo, A.E. 1972. The Warrant Chiefs: Indirect Rule in South-
    Eastern Nigeria, 1891- 1929. Bristol: Western Printing
    Services.
Agba, P.C. 1980. Operation Feed the Nation in Nigeria. Ph.D. disser-
    tation, Indiana University.
Ajayi, J.F.A and B. Ikara 1985. Evolution of Political Culture in
    Nigeria. Ibadan: University Press.
Ake, Claude. 1978. Revolutionary Pressure in Africa. London: Zed
    Press.
_____,1981. A Political Economy of Africa. London: Longman.
_____, 1985. The Political Economy of Nigeria, London and Nigeria,
    Longman Press.

Akeredolu, E. 1975. The Underdevelopment of Indigenous Entrepre-
    neurship in Nigeria. Ibadan: University Press.
Althusser, Louis and Balibar, Etiene. 1970. Reading Capital. London:
    NLB.
Alavi, H. 1972. "The Post-Colonial State." London: "New Left
    Review", 74, July-August. pp.59-82.
Amin, S. 1974. Imperialism and Unequal Development. New York:
    Monthly Review Press.
_____, 1974. Accumulation on a World Scale. Monthly Review
    Press.
_____, 1976. Unequal Development: An Essay on the Formation if
    Peripheral Capitalism. New York: Monthly Review Press.
Amin, S, Giovani, A, Frank G, and Wallerstein I. (1982). Dynamics
    of Global Crisis. New York: Monthly Review Press.
Anikpo, M. 1985. " Mobilizing the Peasantry for National Resistance."
    in G.O. Nwabueze (ed.) Mass Mobilization and National Self-
    Reliance. Port-Harcourt: Faculty of Social Sciences, Univer-
    sity of Port Harcourt, Mimeo.
Aribisala, T.S. 1983. Nigerian's Green Revolution: Achievements,
    Problems and Prospects. Ibadan: NISER Mimeograph series.
Arrighi, G. 1978. "Towards a Theory of Capitalist Crisis." "New
    Left Review", no.111. pp.3-24.
_____, 1982. The Geometry of Imperialism. London: Verso Books.
_____, 1982. "A Crisis of Hegemony," in S.Amin et al. (eds.) Dy
    namics of Global Crisis. New York: Monthly Review Press.
Auer, P., ed. 1981. Energy and the Developing Nations. New York:
    Pergamon Press.
Ayres, R.C. 1983. Banking on the Poor. Cambridge, Mass: MIT Press.
Badru, P. 1982 "Aspects of Rural Transformation in the Sociology of
    Development: The Role of the Military in Land Reform in
    Nigeria". Unpublished Msc.dissertation, London School of
    Economics, London England.
_____, 1984. "Oil Revenue and the Rural-Urban Dichotomy in
    Nigerian Development Experience." "Journal of African Rural
    and Urban Studies."
_____, 1987. "Marital Forms Among the Ijaw People of South
    Eastern Nigeria". Atlanta: "Heritage Magazine", Issue No.1.
    pp. 25-27

_____, 1993. International Capital and Rural Development in the
Third World: The Case of World Bank's Funded Agricultural
Projects in Southeast Nigeria. Ann Arbor: University of
Michigan Micro-film series.

Baran, P. 1952. "On the political Economy and Backwardness."
Manchester School of Economic and Social Studies, 20:66-
84.

Barker, J. (ed.), 1984. The Politics of Agriculture in Africa. London:
Sage Publications.

Bates, R. H. 1974. "Ethnic competition and Modernization Contemporary Africa." "Comparative Political Studies", Vol.6 No.4.

_____,1974. Pattern of Uneven Development: Causes and Conse-
quences in Zambia. Denver, Colorado: University of Denver
Press.

_____, 1981. Markets and State in Tropical Africa. Berkeley:,
University of California press.

Barrows, Walter L. 1976. "Ethnic Diversity and Political Instability in
Black Africa." "Comparative Political Studies", Vol. 9,
No. 2.

Beckman, B. 1982. "Whose State? State and Capitalist Development
in Nigeria." Review of African Political Economy (ROAPE),
10: 60-73.

_____, 1985. " Bakolori: peasants versus the state and capital". "
Nigerian Journal of Political Science." Vol.4 (1-2), pp.76-
104.

Beneria, Lourdes, and Gita Sen. "Accumulation, reproduction and
women's role in economic development: "Boserup revisited"
"Signs", vol.7, no.2 (winter 1981): 279-298.

Beneria, Lourdes and Shelley Feldman. editors, 1992. Unequal
burden: economic crises, persistent poverty, and women's work,
Boulder: Westview Press, 1992.

Bentham, Jeremy. 1960. Fragment on Government. Oxford: Basil
Blackwell.

Berg, E. 1981. Accelerated Development in Sub-Saharan Africa: An
Agenda for Action. Washington, D.C. World Bank.

Bernstein, H. 1976. "African Peasantries: A Theoretical Framework."
"Journal of Peasant Studies", Vol. 6, No. 4. pp.421-443.

Bigman, L. 1993. History and Hunger in West Africa. Westport,
Connecticut: Greenwood Press.

Block, F. 1977. The Origins of the International Economic Disorder.
    New York: Oxford Press.

Boserup, Esther. 1970. The role of women in economic development,
    New York: St. Martin's Press.

Brett, E.A. 1985. The World Economy Since the War: The Politics
    of Uneven Development. New York: Praeger Books.

Browsberger, W. 1983. "Development and Governmental Corruption
    in Nigeria: Materialism and Political Fragmentation in
    Nigeria." "Journal of Modern African Studies", 21, 2,
    pp.215-233.

Buestecker, T. 1978. Distortions or Development: Contending Perspec-
    tives on Multinational Corporations. Massachusetts: MIT
    press.

Cardoso, F.H. 1972. Dependency and Underdevelopment in Latin
    America. New York: Random House.

Carter, April. 1971. The Political Theory of Anarchism. London:
    Routledge and Keegan Paul, 1971.

Christie, R. 1980. "Why Does Capital Need Energy?" In T. Turner
    and P. Nore (eds.), Oil and Class Struggle. London: Zed
    Press.

Chinzea, B. 1985. "The Dialectics of Self-Reliance and Political
    Order in Nigeria." in G.O. Nwabueze (ed.) Mass Mobiliza-
    tion and National Self-Reliance. Port-Harcourt: Faculty of
    Social Sciences, University of Port Harcourt, Mimeo.

Christofferson, L.E. 1980. "The World Bank and Rural Poverty," in
    The World Bank and the World's Poorest. World Bank:
    Washington, D.C.

Clark, J. 1979. Agricultural Production in Rural Yoruba Town. Ph.D.
    dissertation, University of London.

Clawson, P. 1980. "The Internationalization of Capital and Capital
    Accumulation in Iran." In T. Turner and P. Nore, (eds.), Oil
    and Class Struggle. London: Zed Press.

Clegg, Stewart, Boreham, Paul and Dow, Geoff. 1986. Class Politics
    and the economy. London: Routledge and Kegan Paul.

Collier, P. 1981. "Oil and Inequality in Rural Nigeria." ILO World
    Employment Paper (Research Working Paper).

Comte, Augustus. 1953. The Positive Philosophy (2 vols.). New York:
    D.Appleton.

Dahl, Robert. 1967. Democracy in the United States: Promise and Performance. Chicago: Rand McNally, 1967.

_____, 1965. Modern Political Analysis. Cliffs: Prentice-Hall.

_____, 1965. Pluralist Democracy in the United States. New York: The Free Press.

Dennis, C. 1987. " Women and the State in Nigeria: The Case of the Federal Military Government, 1984-85." in Afshar, H (ed.), Women State and Ideology: Studies from Africa and Asia. Albany: SUNY Press.

Dike, A. 1956. The Crown Price of the Niger. Oxford: Oxford University Press.

Domhoff, G.M. 1979. The Powers That Be New York: Vintage Press.

_____, Who Rules America?

Dos Santos, T.1973. "The Crisis of Development Theory and the Problem of Dependence in Latin America", in H. Bernstein (ed.), Underdevelopment and development. Harmondsworth: Penguin Books.

Dunmoye, R.A. 1986. "The State and Peasantry: The Politics of Integrated Rural Development Projects in Nigeria. Unpublished Ph.D. dissertation, University of Toronto, Canada.

_____, 1989. "The Political Economy of Agricultural Production in Africa: State Capital and the Peasantry," Peasant Studies, Vol. 16, No.2. pp.87-104.

ECLA.1990. Economic Report on Africa, 1990. United Nations Economic Commission for Africa: Addis Abba, Ethiopia.

Eicher, C. K. and C. Liedholm, eds. 1970. Growth and the Development of Nigerian Economy. East Lansing: Michigan State University Press.

_____, and D.C. Baker. 1982. Research on Agricultural Development in Sub-Saharan Africa. East Lansing: Michigan State University Press.

Eicher, C. K. and Staatz, J.M. 1990. Agricultural Development in the Third World. Baltimore: The Johns Hopkins University Press.

Eisenstadt, N. 1965. Tradition, Change and Modernity. Englewood, New Jersey: Prentice-Hall.

_____, 1966. Modernization, Protest and Change. New Jersey: Prentice Hall.

Elson, Diane. "How is structural adjustment affecting women?" Development, 1 (1989): 67-74.

Elson, Diane. "From survival strategies to transformation strategies:
    women's needs and structural adjustment." in Lourdes Beneria
    and Shelley Feldman, editors, Unequal burden: economic
    crises, persistent poverty, and women's work. Boulder:
    Westview Press, 1992, 26-48.
Emmanuel, A. 1972. Unequal Exchange. New York: MRP.
Evans, P. 1979 Dependent Development: The Alliance of Multina-
    tional, State, and Local Capital in Brazil. Princeton, New
    Jersey: Princeton University Press.
Falola, T. and Julius Ihonvbere. 1985. The Rise and Fall of Nigeria's
    Second Republic. London: Zed Press.
FAO.1976, Perspective Study on Agricultural Development in the
    Sahelian Countries, 1975-1990. 3 Vols. Rome.
Feder, E. 1976. "The New World Bank Program for Self-Liquidation
    of Third World Peasantry," Journal of Peasant Studies 3: 343-
    54.
Federal Republic of Nigeria. 1962. First National Plan, 1962-1968.
    Lagos: Ministry of Finance.
_____,1970. Second National Plan, 1970-1974. Lagos, Nigeria:
    Ministry of Finance.
_____,1975. Third National Plan, 1975-1980. Lagos, Nigeria:
    Ministry of Finance.
_____, 1980. Fourth National Plan, 1981-1985. Lagos, Nigeria:
    Ministry of Finance.
Federici, Silvia. 1990. "The debt crisis, Africa and the new enclosures."
    Midnight Notes 10, pp. 10-17.
Fieldhouse, D.H. 1986. Black Africa, 1945-86; Economic
    Decolonization and Arrested Development. London: Allen
    and Unwin.
Frank, A.G. 1966. "The Development of Underdevelopment," Monthly
    Review 18, (No.4).
_____, 1967. Capitalism and Underdevelopment in Latin America.
    New York: Monthly Review Press.
Frank, A.G. 1974. The Development of Underdevelopment. New York:
    Monthly Review Press.
_____, 1980. Crisis in the Third World. New York: Monthly Re
    view Press.
Furtado, C. 1965. "Development and Stagnation in Latin America: A

Structural Approach." Studies in Comparative Development, 1 No. 11.

_____, 1970. Economic Development of Latin America, Cambridge: Cambridge Press.

_____, 1973. "The Concept of External Dependence in the Study of Underdevelopment" in C.K. Wilber (ed.), The Political Economy of Development and Underdevelopment. New York: Random House.

Gallaher, M. 1991. Rent Seeking and Economic Growth in Africa, Boulder, Colorado: Westview Press.

Gamble, Andrew. 1981. An Introduction to Modern Social and Political Thought London. Macmillan.

Garba, Joe. 1982. Revolution in Nigeria: Another View. London: African Books.

_____, 1995. Fractured History. Trenton: Songay Books.

Gbulie, Ben. 1982. Nigeria's Five Majors. Africana Educational Publishers.

George, Susan. 1992. The Debt Boomerang: How Third World Debt Harms Us All. Boulder: Westview Press.

Gittinger, J. P.1989. Economic Analysis of Agricultural Projects. Baltimore, John Hopkins University Press.

Graf, W. D. 1988. The Nigerian State. London: James Currey.

Griffin, K. 1972. The Green Revolution: An Economic Analysis. Harmondsworth: Penguin Books.

Gutkind et al. 1976. The Political Economy of Contemporary Africa. Beverly Hills, California: Sage Press.

Harris, J. 1982. Rural Development : Theories of Peasant Economy and Agrarian Change. London: Hutchinson University Library.

Harrison, Frank. 1983. The Modern State. Montreal: Black Rose Books.

Hart, K. 1982. The Political Economy of West Africa Agriculture. London: Cambridge University Press.

Held, David. (ed.). 1983. States and Society. Oxford: Martin Robertson.

Helleiner, G. 1966. Peasant Agriculture, Government, and Economic Growth in Nigeria. Homewood ILL: R.D.Irwin.

_____, 1986. Africa and the IMF. Washington: IMF-publications.

_____, 1981. Essays in Trespassing: Economic to Politics and Beyond. New York: Cambridge University Press.

Heyer, J. and G. Williams, eds. 1981. Rural Development in Tropical

Africa. London: Macmillan Press.

Hirscman, A.O. 1958. The Strategy of Economic Development. New Haven: Yale University Press.

Hobbes, Thomas. 1968. Leviathan. Harmondsworth: Penguin.

Holloway, John and Picciato, S. (eds.). 1979. State and Capital. London: Edward Arnold.

Huntington, S. P. 1957. The Soldier and the State: The Theory of Politics of Civil-Military Relations. Cambridge, MA: Harvard University Press.

_____, 1968. Political Order in Changing Society. New Haven: Yale University Press.

_____, 1991. Third Wave Democratization in the Late Twentieth Century. Norman: University of Oklahoma Press.

Hutchful, E. 1985. "Texaco Funiwa-5 Oil Blowout, Rivers State, Nigeria." Journal of African Marxists, No. 7. pp.51-62.

_____, 1989. The IMF and Ghana: A Confidential Report, London, Zed Press.

Hyden, G. 1980. Beyond Ujamaa: Underdevelopment and the Uncaptured Peasantry. London: Hienemann.

_____, 1983. No Shortcut to progress: African Development Management in Perspective. Berkeley: University of California Press.

Ihimodu, I. 1991. "Agricultural Policy", in Ben Turok (ed.). IFAA Conference Papers on the African Crisis

Ihonvbere, J. & Shaw, Timothy. 1988. Towards a Political Economy of Nigeria. Aldershot: Avebury Press.

Ikoku, S.G. 1980. Building the New Nigeria. A Collection of Essays. Enugu: Fourth Dimension.

_____, 1985. Nigeria's Fourth Coup: Options for Modern State hood. Enugu: Fourth Dimension.

Iyegha, D.A. 1988. Agricultural Crisis in Africa: The Nigerian Experience. Lanham, Maryland: University Press of America.

Jemibewon, David, M. 1978. A Combatant in Government. Ibadan: Heinemann.

Jessop, Bob. 1982. The capitalist State. Oxford: Martin Robertson.

Jorgenson, D.W. 1961. "Development of a Dual Economy", Economic Journal 72 (June):309-34.

Joseph, Peter. 1996. Wole Soynka and the Nigerian Reich: A Review of The Open Sore of a Continent. Paper presented at the ASA meeting in San Francisco, November 23-26, 1996 and forth coming in the January 1997 issue of Journal of Democracy.

Kautsky, K. 1889. The Agrarian Problem. London: Frank Cass.

Kilby, P. 1945-1966. Industrialization in an Open Society -Nigeria.

Laclau, E. 1971. 'Feudalism and Capitalism in Latin America', New Left Review, 67 (May-June 1971). pp.19-38.

_____, 1977. Politics and Ideology in Marxist Theory of Capitalism, London, New Left Books.

Lehman, D., ed. 1974. Agrarian Reform and Agrarian Reformism. London: Faber.

Lele, U and Agarwal, M. 1989. Smallholder and Large Scale Agriculture in Africa: Are There Trade Offs Between Growth and Equity. MADAI Project. Washington: World Bank.

Lenin, V. I. 1966. Imperialism: The Highest Stage of Capitalism. New York: Bantam Books.

_____, 1965. The State and Revolution. Peking: Foreign Languages Press.

Lewis, A. 1955. "Economic Development With Unlimited Labor Supply." Manchester School of Economic and Social Studies, 22(2):139-91.

_____, 1978. The Evolution of the International Economic Order. Princeton: Princeton University Press.

Lewis, Peter. 1993. "Endgame in Nigeria: The Politics of a Failed Transition," African Affairs (93), 323-340.

Leys, C. 1975. Underdevelopment in Kenya, London, Heineman.

Lipton, M. 1976 Why Poor People Stay Poor: Urban Bias in World Development, Cambridge, Mass: Harvard University Press.

Locke, John. 1952. The Second Treatise of Government. Indianapolis: Bobbs Merril.

Macpherson, C.B. 1962. The Political Theory of Possessive Individualism. London: Oxford University Press.

_____, 1975. Democratic Theory. Oxford: Clarendon Press.

Madiebo, A.A. 1980. The Nigerian Revolution and the Biafran War. Enugu: Fourth Dimension.

Manley, M. 1980. "Message to the South-North Conference on the International Monetary System and the New International Order," Development Dialogue (2). pp.4-6.

Marcuse, Herbert. 1960. Reason and Revolution. Boston: Beacon Press

Martin, Michel, 1983. "Corporate Interests and Military Rule." in
    Williams, G., 1982, (ed.) Sub-Saharan Africa.
Martin, G.W. (ed.). 1990. Semiperipheral States in the World-Economy.
    Westport, Connecticut: Greenwood Press.
Marx, Karl. 1971. Capital Vol. I. New York: International Publishers.
_____, 1972a. The Class Struggles in France. Moscow: Interna
    tional Publishers.
_____, 1977. Contribution to the Critique of Political Economy.
    Moscow: Progress Publisher.
_____,and Engels, F. 1973. Selected Works. Moscow: Progress
    Publisher.
Maurice, D. 1972. Political Economy and Capitalism. Greenwood Press:
    Greenwich, Connecticut.
McClleland, R. 1977, The Achieving Society. Prentice-Hall: New York.
McNamara, R. 1973. Address to the World Bank's Board of Gover
    nors. Washington, D.C.
Meillassoux, Claude. 1975. Maids, Meals and Money: Capitalism and
    the Domestic Community, Cambridge: Cambridge University
    Press.
Michels, Robert. 1962. Political Parties. New York: The Free Press.
Mies, Maria. 1984. "Capitalism and subsistence: rural women in India's
    Development." Journal of the Society for International
    Development, Rome 4, pp. 18-25.
Miliband, Ralph. 1973. The State in Capitalist Society. London:
    Quartet.
_____, 1977. Marxism and Politics. Oxford: Oxford University Press.
_____, 1965. "Marx and the State." in Socialist Register.
_____, 1972. "Reply to Nicos Poulantzas." in Robin Blackburn (ed.),
    Ideology in Social Science. Glasgow: Montana Collins.
_____, 1973. "Poulantzas and the Capitalist State", New Left Re
    view, No.82, November-December, 1973.
Mill, John Stuart. 1947. On Liberty (New York: Appleton-Century
    Crofts).
Mills, C.W. 1959. The Power Elite. New York; Oxford University Press.
    Mosca, Gaetano, The Ruling Class (New York: McGraw-Hill,
    1939).
_____, 1986. Patriarchy and Accumulation on a World Scale: Women
    in the International Division of Labour. London: Zed Press.
_____, Claudia von Werlhof; and Veronika Bennholdt-Thomsen.

1988. Women, The Last Colony. London: Zed Press.
Mistry, P. 1990. The Present Role of the World Bank in Africa. London, IFAA.
Nabudere, D. 1978. The Political Economy of Imperialism. London: Zed Press.
Nelson, H.D. 1981. Nigeria: a Country Study. Washington: American University's Foreign Area Study
Nnoli, Okwudiba. 1978. Ethnic Politics in Nigeria. Enugu: Fourth Di mension.
———, 1981. Path to Nigerian Development. London: Zed Press.
Nzimiro, Ikenna. 1972. Studies in Ibo Political Systems: Chieftaincy and Politics in Four Nigerian States. London: Frank Cass.
———, 1979. The Nigerian Civil War: A Study in Class Conflict. Enugu: Fourth Dimension.
Obasanjo, O. 1981. My Command: An Account of the Nigerian Civil War. London: Heinemann.
O'Connor, J. 1984. Accumulation Crisis. New York: Basil Blackwell.
Offe, Clauss. 1984. The Contradictions of the Welfare State. Cam bridge : MIT Press.
Okigbo, P.N.C. 1989. National Development Planning in Nigeria, 1902-92. London: James Currey
Olatunbosun, M. 1975. Nigeria's Neglected Rural Majority. Ibadan: Oxford University Press.
Olayide, S. 1972. "Agriculture in the federal republic of Nigeria", in O. Oyediran (ed.), Survey of Nigerian Affairs.
Olorunsola, Victor. 1972. The Politics of Cultural Sub-Nationalism in Africa. New York: Doubleday.
Onimade, B. 1982. Imperialism and Underdevelopment in Nigeria. London: Zed Books.
———, 1983. Multinational Corporations in Nigeria. Ibadan: Uni- versity Press.
———, 1988. A Political Economy of the African Crisis. London: Zed Press.
———, 1989. The IMF, World Bank and Africa. London: IFAA and Zed Press.
———, 1989. The IMF, World Bank and the African Debt Crisis. London: IFAA and Zed Press.
Othman, H. 1990. Alternative Development Strategy for Africa. London: IFAA (Institute for Africa Alternatives).

Othman, S. and Williams, G.1995. "Politics, Power and Democracy in
    Nigeria."Paper presented at the conference on Transitions in
    West Africa: Towards 2,000 and Beyond, held at the Univer-
    sity of Central Lancashire, Preston, UK, 1-3 September.
Oyewole, Major Fola. 1977. Reluctant Rebels. London: Rex Collings.
Oyinbo, John. 1971. Nigeria: Crisis and Beyond. London: Knight.
Paige, J. 1975. Agrarian Revolution: Social Movements and Export
    Agriculture in the Underdeveloped World. New York:
    Macmillan.
Panther-Brick, K., ed. 1978. "The Political Transformation of
    Nigeria." in Soldiers and Oil. London: Frank Cass.
Payer, C. 1986. The World Bank: A Critical Analysis. New York:
    Monthly Press Review.
Petras, J. 1978. Critical Perspectives on Imperialism and Social Class
    in the Third World. New York: New Left Books.
Petras, James and Morris Morley, 1990. US hegemony under siege.
    London and New York: Verso.
Piji, K. 1984. The Making of an Atlantic Ruling Class. London: Verso
    Press.
Post, K. 1977. "Peasantization in Western Africa." In P. Gutkind and
    Watterman, eds., African Social Studies: A Radical Reader.
    New York: Monthly Review Press.
Poulantzas, N. 1973. Political Power and Social Classes. London:
    Sheedward Press.
_____, 1975. Classes in Contemporary Capitalism. London: New
    Left Books.
_____, 1972. "The Problem of the Capitalist State." in Robin
    Blackburn (ed.). Ideology in Social Sciences. Glasgow:
    Fontana Collins.
_____,"The Capitalist State: Reply to Miliband and Laclau". New
    Left Review , No.95, January-February, 1976).
Pratt, R.C. 1983. "The Global Impact of the World Bank," in Jill Torrie
    (ed.), Banking on Poverty: The Global Impact of the IMF and
    World Bank. Toronto: Between the Line Press.
Prebisch, R. 1959. "Commercial Policy in the Underdeveloped Coun-
    tries." American Economic Review, 64 (May):251-273.
Ranis, G. 1964. The Development of the labor Surplus Economy: Theory
    and Policy. Homewood, ILL.: Richard D. Irwin.

Rodney, W. 1972. How Europe Underdeveloped Africa. London: Beacon Books.

Rostow, W. 1963. The Stages of Growth: A Non-Communist Mani festo. Cambridge University Press: England.

Rutham, V.W. 1990. "Models of Agricultural Development." in Eicher, C.K. et al. Agricultural Development in the Third World. Baltimore: Johns Hopkins University Press.

Sahlins, M. 1977. Neo-authoritarianism and the Problem of Legiti macy. Stockholm: Raben and Sjogren (Hist.).

Schatz, S. P. 1977. Nigerian Capitalism. Berkeley: UCLA Press.

Seidman, A., et al. 1986. Aid and Development, Trenton, AWP.

Shanim, T. (ed.). 1971. Peasants and Peasant Societies London: Penguine Books.

Shaw, T. and Adedeji, A.(eds.). 1988. Economic Crisis in Africa: African Perspectives in Development Problems and Potentials. Boulder, Colorado: L. Reinner Publishers.

Shiva, Vandana. 1989. "Development: the "new colonialism," in Development, (Journal of the Society for International Development, Rome) 1, pp. 84-87.

Stavenhagen, R. 1973. "Classes, Colonialism, and Acculturation.", in Studies in Comparative International Development, Vol.1, No.6. pp.53-77

Suleiman, M. (ed.) 1991. Africa Vol II: Environment and Women, IFAA.

Szentes, T. 1971. The Political Economy of Underdevelopment. Budapest: Hungarian Academy of Sciences.

Szymanski, Albert. 1978. The capitalist State and the Politics of class. Cambridge: Winthrop.

Tanzer, M. 1980. "Oil Exploration Strategies: Alternative Strategics for the Third World." In T. Turner and P. Nore (eds.), Oil and Class Struggle. London: Zed Press.

_____, 1980. The Race for Resources. New York: Monthly Review Press.

Taylor, R.T. 1988. Hot Money and the politics of Development. London: Zed Press.

Trager, L. and Osinulu, C. 1991. "New women's organizations in Nigeria: one response to structural adjustment," in Christina H. Gladwin (ed.) Structural adjustment and African women farmers. Gainesville: University of Florida Press, 1991, pp. 339-358.

Turner, T. 1978. "Commercial Capitalism and the 1975 Coup." In K. Panther-Brick, ed., Soldiers and Oil. London: Frank Cass.

———, 1980. "Nigeria: Imperialism, Oil Technology and the Comprador State." Oil and Class Struggle. London: Zed Press.

———, and P. Nore, eds. 1980. Oil and Class Struggle. London: Zed Press.

———, and Badru, P. 1985. "Oil and Instability: Class Contradictions and the 1983 Coup", in Journal of African Marxists, London, England. pp.4-34.

Ukpu, U. 1979. Ethnic Minority Problems in Nigerian Politics 1960-65. Upsalla: Studia Historica Upsaliensia 88.

United Bank for Africa, 1990. Monthly Business and Economic Digest. (Various issues, 1990-1992. Lagos: Nigeria).

Usman, Bala. 1979. For the Liberation of Nigeria. London: Beacon.

———, 1982. Political Repression in Nigeria. Kano: Bala Mohammed Memorial Committee.

Usman, Bala. 1988. The Manipulation of Religion in Nigeria, 1977-1987. Kaduna: Vanguard Press.

Wallerstein, I. 1974. The Origin of the Modern World System. New York: Monthly Review Press.

———, 1979. The Capitalist World Economy. New York: Cambridge University Press.

———, 1984. The Politics of the World- Economy: The states, the Movements, and the Civilizations. Cambridge: Cambridge University Press.

———, 1986. The Three Stages of Africa Involvement in the World Economy. Trenton, New Jersey: Third World Press.

Watts, M. 1987. State, Oil and Agriculture in Nigeria. Berkeley: University of California Press.

Wilber, C.K. 1965. "Development and Stagnation in Latin America: a Structural Approach", Studies in Comparative Development, 1 (No.11).

———, 1970. Economic Development of Latin America. Cambridge: Cambridge Press.

———, 1973. The Political Economy of Development and Underdevelopment. New York: Random House.

William, G. 1980. State and Society in Nigeria. Nigeria: Afrographical Publishers.

_____, 1987. "The World Bank in Rural Nigeria: A review of the World Bank's Nigerian Agricultural Sector", Occasional papers. St. Peter's College, Oxford.

_____, (Undated) 'Why is there no Agrarian Capitalism in Nigeria? 'occasional papers, University of Ibadan, Nigeria.

_____, 1981. "The World Bank and the Peasant Problem," in Rural Development in Africa, eds. P. Heyer et al. New York: St. martin Press.

World Bank's Document No.1525-UNI, 1978: Appraisal of Nucleus Estate/Smallholder Oil Palm Project in Rivers State, Nigeria.

World Bank. 1983. Sub-Saharan Africa-Progress Report on Development: Prospects and Programmes. Washington.

_____, 1981. Accelerated Development in Sub-Saharan Africa.

_____,1989. Sub-Saharan Africa: From Crisis to Sustainable Growth. Washington D.C.

_____, Special Memorandum on the Agricultural Sector in Nigeria, Vol.I, June 15, 1984.

_____, 1990. Making Adjustment Work for the Poor. Washington, DC.

_____, 1986. World Debt Tables. Washington, DC.

_____, 1990. Financing Adjustment with Growth in Sub-Saharan Africa, 1986-1990. Washington, DC.

_____, 1990. Social Indicators of Development 1990. Washington, DC.

_____, 1990. Annual Report: Trends in Developing Economies. Washington, DC.

, 1991. World Development Report. The Challenge of Development. Washington, DC.

_____, 1991. Annual Report. Washington, DC.

_____, 1991. Global Economic Prospects and the Developing Countries. Washington, DC.

Index